Sex and the Single Mother
Romance and Relationships in the Eighties

Sex
and the
Single Mother

*Romance and Relationships
in the Eighties*

Dawn B. Sova

Dodd, Mead & Company   New York

No part of this book may be reproduced in any form
without permission in writing from the publisher.
Published by Dodd, Mead & Company, Inc.
71 Fifth Avenue
New York, N.Y. 10003
Distributed in Canada by
McClelland and Stewart Limited, Toronto
Manufactured in the United States of America
Designed by Marilyn E. Beckford

First Edition

1 2 3 4 5 6 7 8 9 10

Library of Congress Cataloging-in-Publication Data

Sova, Dawn B.
Sex and the single mother.

Includes index.
1. Single parents—Sexual behavior. 2. Interpersonal
relations. 3. Parent and child. I. Title.
HQ759.915.S66 1987   306.8'743   86–24183
ISBN 0-396-08860-0

This book is dedicated to
my patient and loving son,
Robby Gregor

Contents

4
When Does the Mourning End? 42
Widowed—But Still Alive; Living Your Own Life;
Sex and the Widowed Mother; The Men in Your
Life

5
What's Wrong With Being Never-Married? 52
Neither "Unwed" Nor "Illegitimate"; Maintaining
the Image You Choose; Sex and the Never-Married
Mother

6
What Is the Age Gauge? 59
Age and the Availability of Men; Age and the
Sources of Romance; Age and Living
Arrangements; Age and the Influence of Children

7
Are the Men Still the Same? 66
Who Are These Strangers?; What Do Men Want?;
How Do Men View Your Family?

8
What Are Your Choices in Men? 73
The "New Feminist" Man; The "Macho Man";
The "Liberated" Man; The "Sad Sack"; The
"Walking Wounded"; The Gay Male Friend; The
Straight Male Friend; The "Truly Liberated" Man

9
Where Will You Meet Men? 89
Planning Your "Debut"; The Divorced
"Debutante"; The Widowed "Debutante"; Looking
for Love in All the Right Places; Taking the
Comfortable Approach; Formal Matchmaking;
Single Parents' Groups; The Dating Services;
Personal Ads

Acknowledgments

This book has come to life under the sensitive and intelligent editing of Jerry Gross, Senior Editor at Dodd, Mead & Company, whose perceptive questions and insightful suggestions helped to give form to the idea. I am very grateful for his time and his guidance.

My appreciation goes out to my agent, Guy Kettelhack, for encouraging me and having faith in me.

I am also deeply indebted to Dr. Shdema Goodman, Dr. Victor Solomon, Dr. Burton Schucker, and Dr. Marge Steinfeld for speaking with me and for offering their professional expertise to the single mothers who read this book.

A great debt is also owed to the hundreds of single mothers and men who date single mothers who were willing to share their experiences with me. I believe that example is the best teacher, and they provided me with many examples from which I, too, learned.

To Macarthur Nickles, Director of the Garfield (New Jersey) Public Library, I extend my thanks for providing his enthusiastic encouragement of the topic and suggestions. I also extend my thanks to Gale Zimmer and Robert Nedswick, as well as Penny Kaplan and Mary Burdick, of the Maurice M. Pine Free Public Library (Fair Lawn, New Jersey) for locating organized answers for my often disorganized questions.

My family receives the most deeply felt gratitude, for they have shared my many joys and my fears during my eight years as a single mother.

I can never fully express how much I appreciate the love and concern of my son, Robby Gregor, whose birth on Mother's Day 1977, made me a most happy mother.

Nor can I ever truly repay the love, support, and understanding of my parents, Emil and Violet Sova, who taught me what parenting truly means.

Last, but definitely not least, I want to thank my sister, Millicent Petrullo, and my niece, Sammantha Petrullo, for making life easier for my son and me during my early years as a single mother.

Preface

There are over six million divorced, widowed, and never-married mothers in this nation who are raising a total of 12.7 million children under the age of eighteen. There are millions more single mothers whose children have grown and left their homes but not their lives. Single mothers range in age from teenagers to women in their seventies. Their children may be infants or middle-aged. Whatever their age or the ages of their children, all single mothers must confront the fact that they are both mothers and women.

You have every right to romance and sexual pleasure, and you can enjoy intimate relationships without compromising your role as a mother even if your ultimate aim isn't marriage. Most guides to single parenting tend to ignore this fact and focus instead on the dating and mating that will provide both male and female single parents with a replacement for the absent parent. Ignored is the fact that most single parents (over 90 percent) are mothers and the fact that although many single mothers do want to remarry, others seek male friends, lovers, and confidants, as well as surrogate fathers for their children—but not necessarily husbands for themselves. These guides also fail to look at romantic relationships from the perspective of your children.

Sex and the Single Mother is the first guide to tell the single mother what she needs to know in order to succeed in both romance and motherhood. In writing this book, Dawn Sova, herself a single mother for eight years, has provided a much-needed guide for the single mother of every age who wants a fulfilling romantic life without compromising her relationship with her children. Women who have formed successful relationships, as well as men who date single mothers, have shared their stories of pain and love in these pages. Professionals who work with single mothers and their children have shared their expertise in this area and provide valuable guidance.

In *Sex and the Single Mother,* you will learn to judge when the time is "right" to begin dating, how to select your partners, where to meet and to mate, and how to handle your sexual relationships. You will learn to identify the dilemmas faced by your children and how to help them to cope with their feelings.

In addition, *Sex and the Single Mother* also dares to talk about the topics that most single parenting books avoid: how to select the sexual arrangements that *you* want; who are today's men; why the younger man is sometimes the best choice; how to avoid sexual and other abuse of your children by the men in your life; what men who date single mothers say and feel; why your age affects your style of romance; and how you can be celibate and still sexy.

With its practical advice and the straightforward examples of single mothers of all ages who have achieved successful romantic relationships, *Sex and the Single Mother* is a valuable, commonsense guide for every single mother who loves and values her children but who also wants romance in her life.

Burton Schucker, Ph.D.
Counseling and Psychotherapy Center
Fair Lawn, New Jersey

Introduction

Being a single mother isn't easy. I know. My eight years as a single mother have simultaneously been the most satisfying and the most frustrating years that I have ever known. In that time, I have gone from my late twenties to my mid-thirties, while my son has grown from a fourteen-month-old infant to a sturdy preadolescent.

The years in between have made us both come to rely on each other, and they have given us the strength to learn to rely on ourselves. During these years, we have had the usual difficulties that single-mother-headed families face. There always seems to be too little money and too little time to do the things that we need to do, and too much guilt over not being able to do the things that we want to do.

More prominent in my mind, however, are the pleasures of those years. I have watched my son grow, and I have answered his questions, calmed his fears, and acted as his teacher. He is a very important part of my life.

In those years, I have also dated various men in relationships that have lasted from only a few weeks to a few years. Some of these men have remained friends to my son and to me, while others have dropped completely out of our lives. Some of the relationships have been satisfying, others have not. All of them, however, have included my son to one degree or another.

Much has been written about single mothering and about the plight of the divorced, widowed, or never-married mothers who make up the nebulous group known as "single mothers."

To a great extent, the emphasis has been upon learning to cope—with financial difficulties, guilt, time pressures, and the many other daily problems that plague our lives. Very little has been written about the pleasures of being a single mother. And there are pleasures.

Sex and the Single Mother has been written to correct that lack. There is more to being a single mother than just suffering and coping.

You are a single mother, but you are also a woman. This is sometimes difficult to remember when we see that much of what is written about us seems to deal only with the dark side of being a single mother. We are advised as either one or the other, either as a single mother or as a woman, but rarely as the whole person that is a woman who is also a single mother.

Because of this division of our roles by the media, many single mothers have come to believe either that romance and relationships are impossible for us or that they must of necessity exclude our children. These are myths that the nearly four hundred women who agreed to talk to me about their sexual and romantic relationships refute.

Women everywhere have found that they can pleasurably combine both romance and mothering without cheating either, as long as they are honest about both and as long as they don't compromise their relationships with their children.

Sex and the Single Mother doesn't deal with the problems that concern most books for single mothers, and it isn't written from the standpoint of a professional who exists outside of the single mother situation. It is written *for* single mothers, based on information obtained *from* single mothers who have experienced successful sexual and romantic relationships.

Men who date single mothers have also offered their experiences, advice, and warnings for single mothers who want to enjoy successful and satisfying sexual and romantic relationships. Most important of all, the children of single mothers whose stories appear in this book have a lot to tell us about their fears and feelings when their mothers date.

In addition to discussing when to begin dating and where to find suitable partners, this book focuses on a very important member of your life—your child. Everything that you do indirectly or directly influences your child's happiness and well-being. Your ups and downs in meeting and mating men will also have an effect on them. Because of this, several chapters are devoted to preparing your children for your dating and to making them comfortable with your arrangements.

As you have gathered by this point, *Sex and the Single Mother* is a guide to living and loving as a happy and fulfilled single mother in the 1980s. Single mothers, the men they date, their children, and the experts in such relationships, have been generous in their advice and in their warnings.

There are significant differences between *Sex and the Single Mother* and other books that have touched on the topic. Rather than view sex and romance as addenda to more dominant concerns with the daily problems of life as a single mother, this book gives its full attention to romantic relationships. The who, what, where, and why, as well as the why not, of living and loving as a single mother are explored.

Another significant difference is that *Sex and the Single Mother* is concerned with all single mothers. It does not limit itself to only the divorced, only the widowed, or only the never-married. For this reason, all ages of single mothers were interviewed for the book, and you will find that it is not only the single mother of small children who may need a little advice about her private affairs.

There is one other very important point that *Sex and the Single Mother* makes that cannot be emphasized too strongly. The men that you date should be carefully screened—if not for your own safety, then for the sake of your children. You may feel that a chapter about the sexual or physical abuse of children would be inappropriate in a book about meeting and mating. In this case, it is not only appropriate but vital, because more than one single mother has allowed a romantic obsession to blind her to her lover's dangerous actions toward her child.

Being a single mother can be a wonderful and love-filled experience with your children. It can be made even more rich and fulfilling when the right romantic relationship becomes a part of your life.

1

Ready to Take a Chance on Romance?

Romance. The word conjures up visions of long-stemmed roses and soft candlelight, intimate dinners and long walks in the moonlight, passionate evenings and sensual pleasures. And we look at romance as something that happens to other women, not the single mother who struggles by day with professional responsibilities and by night with "mothering" duties.

Some of us protest that our whirlwind schedules leave little enough time for the occasional bubble bath, let alone a relationship with all of the romantic trimmings. Even sadder, many of us avoid romance because we are afraid. We are afraid of failing. We are afraid of how the relationship will affect our children. We are afraid that we cannot have a successful romantic relationship *and* be good mothers to our children.

Most of us have heard horror stories from our friends whose romantic relationships have foundered or whose children have been emotionally or physically damaged by their mother's romantic partner. Too often we are just too frightened to take a chance on romance. As a result, we work hard at discouraging men who try to initiate relationships—and we cheat both ourselves and our children in the process.

When is the right time to begin a romantic relationship?

"You'll know when the time is right," says Dr. Shdema Goodman, a licensed psychologist in private practice and the founder of the Biofeedback Institute and Stress Management

Center of New Jersey. "The 'right' person will produce the 'right' feeling in you when you are ready to reach for romance once again. Whether it is for one night or for the rest of your life, your inner knowing will tell you when you are ready, once more, to take a chance."

If deciding that she is ready for romance is a single mother's own decision, then why do so many single mothers find taking that step to be so difficult? The reasons vary as widely as the women involved.

- The trauma of widowhood or a messy divorce may have left you emotionally drained, and romance may take too much effort.
- Juggling work and the needs of your children may take up all of your time.
- Friends and family may make you feel guilty about wanting to become romantically involved again.
- Your fears about testing the waters may prolong your increasingly intense evening relationship with your television set.
- Your children may tell you repeatedly that "life is perfect this way."

Further, how dare you upset everyone's satisfaction with your solitary state by wanting to have a satisfying adult relationship?

For your own sake, you *must* dare, because life changes and you have a long and potentially wonderful life ahead. You have all of life in which to laugh, to love and to make love, and to enjoy romance. These are not privileges. They are your rights.

- The pain of death or divorce will eventually fade.
- Your life will eventually settle down to a dull roar.
- Friends and family will eventually get back to their own concerns.
- Your children will grow up and away.

You will still have your television set, but that is cold comfort if you spend your life alone.

This doesn't mean that you should immediately rush out and begin to search for the perfect romance and attentive companionship. Instead, take a close look at your life and decide what it is that you want, then go after it.

The Right Time for Romance

"There are no hard and fast rules to tell a woman when it's time to begin dating," notes Dr. Victor Solomon, a clinical psychologist who has worked extensively with single-mother families. "There is no golden rule to follow in planning your new social life. You are the only person who can decide when you are ready to open your life to romance."

The same view is shared by others who counsel single mothers. There is no timetable to follow. Rather, single mothers must decide when to begin dating. That often occurs once the woman herself feels comfortable with the idea.

"Because your experience is unique, your decision to seek out a romantic relationship must also be unique," notes Dr. Marge Steinfeld, a psychotherapist in group practice whose expertise is working with families and adolescents. "Not only will women who have been divorced, widowed, and never-married differ as to the right time for new romance, but differences in romantic readiness also exist depending upon your age, number of children, living arrangements, and other factors that are a part of your specific life."

The "right" time to begin dating varies with every woman, and no one can tell you how you feel. Nonetheless, you should take stock of your feelings and make a point of resuming a social life as soon as possible.

"A woman is 'ready' when she has successfully worked through the grief experience over the death, the divorce, or other loss," suggests Dr. Solomon. "Women should resume a social life as soon as they can comfortably do so. To wait only encourages delay. Patterns develop that are hard to change. If a woman is constantly postponing reentering a social life, she may never get to it. She will just continue to postpone and to delay."

Although following your inner voice is highly recommended, you can't ignore the role that cultural and ethnic taboos must play in your decision. You may feel ready for romance and eager for a sexual relationship after one month of widowhood, but where you live may make "doing your own thing" highly uncomfortable. Not every single mother lives in anonymity in a large and impersonal city. Those who do can more freely follow their inner voice and begin dating however soon they feel ready. For others who live in small towns or old neighborhoods, or who are strongly tied to family or to their religious or ethnic group, such freedom must be tempered by caution.

"I do believe that the single mother has to make her own decisions about romance," observes Dr. Goodman. "Still, there are cultural and social taboos that have to be considered. Your children will be affected by your decision. If your children will suffer because you 'jump the gun' in beginning to date after divorce or being widowed, then it might be better to restrain your desires for a time. I don't believe in suffering needlessly, but you have to consider the comfort of your children, too."

What Role Do Children Play?

How can anyone else tell you how you feel?

They can't. Still, too many single mothers depend upon the opinions of others when deciding if the time has come to begin dating. Well-meaning (and not-so-well-meaning) relatives and friends may make you feel guilty for "depriving" your children of a male figure in their lives; then they may chastise you for enjoying your new relationships. You may be told to "begin living again," but you may also be accused of neglecting your children if you seem to be enjoying life too much!

Certainly, your children, whether toddlers or adults, will express their opinions about your new social life. Don't expect those opinions to always agree with yours, because they often won't.

As Dr. Steinfeld suggests, "There is no 'right' time for children, so you shouldn't 'check in' with them when deciding whether or not the time has come to begin dating."

The decision, instead, is an adult decision that must grow out of your own feelings of readiness to handle a new relationship. Nonetheless, although you shouldn't consult your children in regard to your feelings, their feelings should count.

"Because you and your children operate as a unit, you must take your children's needs into account when you begin dating," recommends Dr. Solomon. "Children don't need a 'right' time to give their mothers permission to begin a social life. In reality, they are always ready. Children love people and they love to interact with people, but they want to feel as if they are important in their own right. Therefore, the mother's dating should be introduced gradually and as a natural activity. If you are comfortable with your decision, your children will sense this and they, too, will become comfortable with Mommy dating."

Your child should not decide whether or not you date. Neither should your child be blamed if you find romance elusive. Sociologist Robert S. Weiss found when writing *Going It Alone* that single mothers frequently blame their children for loneliness and for difficulties in finding the time and the opportunity to seek out romance. Children can become the single mother's scapegoats, and she may often think, "If I didn't have the children, then I could be out having a good time. More men would be interested in me if I had no responsibilities."

The woman who thinks this way may be right. Finding a lover might be easier if life were less complicated. But the reality of the single mother's life is that she is a mother and she owes her children her care and love—not her reproaches.

Sadly, the single mother who often complains about her romantically barren life and bemoans the existence of her children may well be the cause of her own isolation. Such a single mother, you will often find, was a woman whose social life was fairly limited even when she was single and childless. Of course, her reasons then were different: her parents, her job, her health, and so on.

This is not meant to imply that you are to be blamed if you find romance elusive. Not at all. There can be many reasons that romance doesn't just "happen." The lack of opportunity to meet men is a primary reason. However, blaming your children for this lack is hardly fair. Their feelings will be hurt. Your relationship with them will be negatively affected. You will feel guilty.

Just as you should not blame your children for your limited or nonexistent social life, neither should you make them the reason for your dating. "I want a father for my children" is a handy excuse to cover up our own desires for romance and for a sexual partner, if we feel such excuses are needed. They can, however, backfire when both you and your children come to see the man in your life only as a potential "daddy" and not as your lover.

You are better off if you admit to yourself and your children that you choose to date a man because he appeals to the woman in you, not for his future fathering capabilities. In some cases, this reason dominates a woman's thinking. Such capabilities are important, should a relationship evolve into something permanent, but don't make daddy-hunting your sole reason for seeking romance. Your children will eventually grow up and leave both you and the man who would be "Daddy." If his sole source of attraction was his parenting potential, then life alone with him may be a shock.

Traps to Avoid

You will receive mountains of advice as to what is best for you and for your children, but *you* will have to live with your final decision. Why, then, should you allow others to tell you when you are ready?

Have you ever participated in a new activity because others told you that you would love it—then found yourself hating every moment spent in the activity? If so, then you probably realized afterward that you had been acting only on the advice of others without assessing your own feelings about the activity. Had you taken the time to compare the requirements of the activity with your own preferences, you might have waited to participate or put off your decision indefinitely.

The single mother who is thinking about beginning a social life is in very much the same boat when she listens to others.

Miriam's Lesson

Miriam, thirty-seven and the mother of two boys aged eight and ten, learned this lesson the hard way after her husband Jeff died. Widowed after fifteen years of marriage to a man her own age, she grieved deeply over the loss of both her husband and the father of her sons. At the same time that she mourned, Miriam was determined not to withdraw from the world around her and thereby deprive her sons of their remaining parent. She talked with them about their father, planned activities, and worked to create a new life for her changed family.

After a year had passed, both friends and family decided that a decent period of mourning had occurred and that Miriam should begin to look for a man to share her life and to be a father to her sons. Until this point, Miriam had been content with the course that her life had taken since the death of her husband. With her sons in school all day, she had been able to begin teaching again, and she found that she enjoyed being in the classroom. Through her job, Miriam had met other single mothers, and they often went out in groups with their children.

As a single mother, Miriam had also overcome her former reluctance to join in the boys' activities. In the past, her husband had taken the boys to all of their activities since Miriam had felt that it was more appropriate for sons and fathers to join in the mostly athletic events. But now, as her sons' only parent, she felt right at home on the sidelines at youth baseball and basketball games. She even joined other parents, married and unmarried, in transporting the boys, supporting the teams, and planning postgame celebrations.

If you had asked Miriam if she and her sons felt deprived, her answer would have been a resounding "no." The three of them missed her late husband very much, but they were able to construct a new life that was satisfying to all of them. There were many fathers and male coaches in the activities her sons enjoyed, and both Miriam and the boys felt companionable with them.

Friends and family could not leave well enough alone. Her parents argued that she needed a man to support her, in spite of her success in managing in the previous year, and that someone had to be around to protect her against a range of unknown evils. And what of her sons? Shouldn't they have a man in the house?

Miriam's friends argued that she was not getting any younger. Once she reached forty, so the argument went, she would find it very difficult to attract a man. They advised that she would be wise to begin looking now, while she still had a chance.

As her friends and family pressured her at every turn to begin looking for a partner, Miriam's confidence and contentment began to crumble. The activities were fun, and her sons seemed to be enjoying their life, but she began to have doubts. Perhaps she should be doing more for them.

That "more" meant finding a new husband for herself and a new parent for her children. Although she inwardly fought against her decision, Miriam began to accept the invitations of friends and family to meet the parade of "perfect" men that they had culled for her. After several disastrous dinners and enough blind dates to cure anyone, Miriam found the strength to call a halt to the matchmaking.

After sixteen unhappy, boring, or unpleasant dates in two months, during which she had been forced to leave baseball games early and miss a variety of activities with her sons and their friends, Miriam told everyone firmly that she was no longer available for their charity. She had missed the fun that she had experienced with her sons, their friends, and the other parents in their group activities. If she was depriving herself and her children, she asserted, then they would just have to accept that she liked deprivation.

Both family and friends were miffed for a time. Dire predictions that she would live a lonely old age and eventually die alone filtered back to Miriam, who merely shrugged.

"I'm happy now," she told friends. "Why should I worry about what might happen forty years from now? Let me find my own way."

Miriam did find her own way, and happily so. After several years of sharing the transportation of their children and joining in athletic practices and postgame celebrations, Miriam and the father of one of her son's friends were married. The romance had blossomed gradually, over muddied uniforms, equipment-filled cars, dropped pizzas, and spilled sodas. Their children were close in age and shared the same interests, as did the parents.

Could she have been happy with one of the "perfect" men that her family and friends had trotted out for her? They had all been materially successful and available for romance. They may have all been attractive and eligible partners—but for another woman. Although she had tried, Miriam had not really been ready for romantic involvement, even though she had given in to the pressures of both family and friends to make the effort.

Had her resistance to pressure been lower, and had she not been so happily involved in the group activities with her sons, Miriam might have made the mistake of *forcing* herself to become involved with someone. That mistake could have made everyone—Miriam, her sons, and the man—miserable if it had continued into remarriage.

How did it happen for Miriam? Could it happen in the same way for you? Should romance just be allowed to happen— or should the single mother take steps to make it happen?

That depends on you and on whether or not you are ready for romance when the opportunity presents itself. Don't fool yourself by thinking that fate will take care of everything. It can't if you are not ready to see the opportunities for romance along the way.

It is equally important that you don't fool yourself into feeling that you are ready for romance. There are many traps that make us feel that any relationship would be better than our present life alone. Loneliness, economic need, surrender to the expectations of others, the wish to only provide a father for your children, or sexual needs do not individually signal that you are emotionally ready to become involved in an intimate, romantic relationship.

In particular, sexual need may have little to do with a desire for emotional closeness or for the investment of time and effort that a successful romantic relationship requires. Sexual need alone only signals a need for physical involvement, and that doesn't necessarily mean intimacy or a relationship.

How you satisfy this need may differ tremendously from the way in which you signify and act on your readiness for romantic involvement. Women who have learned the difference between feeling a need for sex and being ready for romance view the two as vitally different.

"I won't apologize for myself," asserts Vera, the vivacious divorced mother of an eleven-year-old daughter. "I *know* that I'm not ready to become romantically involved with a man just yet, but my hormones don't want to hear excuses. At times, all I want is a man for an hour. Slam, bam, no last names. Are you shocked? It's not ideal, I'll admit, but when my sexual need speaks loudly, I feel as if I'll go crazy if I don't satisfy that need. A one-night stand, or maybe masturbation, and it's gone. That kind of need is no basis for a relationship, so I don't try to make it one."

What of the other traps that lure some single mothers into feeling that they have no choice but to become romantically involved with someone—anyone? Loneliness can be a seductive trap. Many divorced people, both men and women, complain of loneliness after divorce, but keep in mind that so do many unhappily married people.

For the single mother, however, loneliness can present a more serious problem. After years of being with someone, for better or for worse, many women find themselves unable to cope with being the only adult in the house. They miss having someone else to make the decisions—or to protest their decisions. They miss the accessibility of another adult body, for both sexual and emotional needs. For some, the prospect of facing the holidays as a single mother is the source of extreme anxiety, even when such times are spent at a large family gathering.

"Just being around all of the others, the husbands and wives and the kids who have both parents, makes me feel this dull ache inside," confided forty-six-year-old Gina, a widow with two teenagers. "I cry when I get home and can't help but feel that I should be married, and that there is something wrong with me because I'm not."

Even women who claim to have come to terms with their single status in a world that seems to be peopled by couples admit to feeling a twinge of loneliness now and then when they attend social functions alone or when they run into long-married friends. The cure for such loneliness certainly lies in finding a warm and meaning-filled romantic involvement, but it is no reason for you to rush headlong into the arms of the first available man. And it is not sufficient reason to believe that you are ready for a new relationship.

Economic need also propels too many women into hasty involvements that lead to hasty remarriages and—too frequently—to equally hasty divorces. Money problems are hard to face when you are struggling with little or no financial support. The landlord, utility company, supermarkets, and other stores want to be paid, and many single mothers have the sole responsibility for finding the money. When economic burdens weigh you down, it becomes very easy to fantasize what life would be like with another income. How much more comfortable and stable life could be for you and your children!

Many single mothers find that a man who would be otherwise undesirable suddenly becomes highly interesting when he reveals that he has a stable and well-paying job. Struggle may be heroic, but even the most heroic of single mothers can be worn down by dire economic need.

Still, to make economic need your sole reason for entering a romantic relationship with the hope for a hasty remarriage is dangerous. Unless other reasons are present, you will soon find that the disadvantages of living with someone whom you don't really know or care about can far outweigh the advantages of having your bills paid on time. Economic stability is desirable, but you shouldn't trade yourself in only for its rewards.

Another trap for the single mother who may be hesitant about getting romantically involved is the pressure that others will place on her to "catch a man." While you may be perfectly happy with your single lifestyle and with only casual dates, others will be eager to have you romantically involved and married off as soon as possible. Their intentions are often the very best.

Your parents will worry that you and your children need a man's presence, protection, and income. They will comb their surroundings and enlist the aid of their friends to find available men for you to meet.

Your married friends will alternately envy you and pity you. They will also wrack their brains to find men for you to meet at "informal" (read "highly planned") social events at their homes. Having you safely married once again is the aim of any wife who views you as a sexual threat with her husband, as well as any wife who may wish that she had your present freedom. Of course, there are also those friends who genuinely believe that marriage is the best state, and they genuinely want to help you back into such an arrangement.

Most people will not leave you alone with your contentment, should you want to remain single. Some people will feel uncomfortable when they realize that you can function perfectly well as the sole parent to your children. Your success threatens their need to be married. Others will see you as "brave" and too naive to know what is best for you. So they will force their opinions on you in what can only be called a misguided desire to help you. Still others will view your resistance to marrying as being abnormal.

Any mother who has not remarried after a year can be sure to be subjected to such questions as the following: When are you going to get married again? Why not find a man to share some of the burden? How long do you think men will keep looking? Better get married while you're still young and attractive. Don't you want your children to have a father?

One swipe at the single mother's happiness comes from men who consider her contentment to be a personal rejection of them. The crafty fellow who has been turned down after graciously offering the single mother a chance to enjoy his fascinating company will sneer, "What's the matter with you? Are you one of those women who is turned on only by other women?"

Don't let the questions bother you. More important, don't let these attempts at pressure make you feel that you *have* to become romantically involved. The mildly annoying cajoling of friends and family is usually well intended and can be brushed aside with a good-natured rebuff. Vicious remarks that point out that you're headed over the hill or those like the final question, which seek to make you an object of contempt, deserve no answer at all. They are motivated by envy or feelings of inadequacy on the part of the speaker.

Being "Ready"

How do you know when you are ready for romantic involvement? No time schedule can apply to everyone. There are no agreed-upon rules as to what constitutes a "decent interval" after separation or divorce, and the traditional one year of mourning after death is also frequently ignored. The general relaxation of societal restrictions in other matters also seem to have softened the rules for single mothers.

Rather than deciding that a month, six months, a year, or ten years must pass before a divorced, widowed, or never-married single mother is ready for a romantic relationship, you have to assess how you feel. To do this, you will have to ignore the often liberal advice that family, friends, and strangers will force upon you.

Consider the following questions in making your decision:

1. Do you feel that you have successfully put your old hurts and losses aside so that you can become romantically involved without the ghosts of old relationships intruding?
2. Can you make the time in your life that is necessary for seeking out and nurturing a new romance?

3. Have you taken control of your life and made it clear to friends, family, and children that you will make your own decisions?
4. Have you determined the type of relationship that you desire, and do you know how to achieve it?
5. Do you feel ready to experience the thrill of romance and sexual intimacy?

This last item may well be the most interesting and difficult for you to answer. You may deny vehemently that you miss the romance and sexual excitement of being with a special man.

Admitting to such natural feelings seems to be almost a cause for shame for some single mothers who fear that wanting to be with a man and responding to their completely normal and expected sexual desires are somehow contradictions to the role of mother. They feel that they are somehow cheating their children if they begin to enjoy sexual pleasure again. Such fears are uncalled for. Blocking out the desire for an active and healthy sex life can do more harm than good in your life.

Have you been afraid to admit that you are ready and willing to find a sexy and romantic partner to help you restart life? Or do you instead create for yourself a range of reasonable and "respectable" excuses such as "Everyone says that it's time to go out" or "The children need a male role model"?

You may also have been tempted to hide your readiness for romance behind a barrage of reasons that have little to do with the most important reason of all for seeking out romance— your own need to feel alive, desired, and needed by a man. Rather than make excuses, you should squarely face the fact that a time will come, as it may already have, when you will want to laugh, flirt, joke, cuddle, and make love with an adult male who views you as a desirable adult female. When that time comes, then you will know that you are ready to take a chance on romance once again.

"It wasn't a sudden realization, and I didn't feel any great inspiration," recalls Terry, a forty-one-year-old widow with one son. "Instead, I gradually felt myself coming to life again and beginning to notice the broad shoulders on one man, the distinguished gray hair of another, and the lively banter of others. My evenings spent with my fourteen-year-old son began to take on a less frantic air, and we both began to enjoy them more as

I relaxed and played with the idea of beginning to date. I had healed over the ten months since my husband's death, and with healing had come a willingness to take a chance on loving again. When I began to find men attractive, when I actually began to notice men again, I knew that I was ready to become romantically involved."

Are you ready for romance? You can become ready by taking control of your life and deciding when and with whom you want to have a relationship. As a single mother, you have the responsibility for the well-being of yourself and of your children. While you will have many admirers in regard to whatever decision you make, you should also expect to have your share of detractors.

Most people seem to feel that single mothers are inadequate, and they want to see you married and "protected" as soon as possible. Others who see you carrying on successfully may feel threatened by your success as a single mother, and they will also want to see you married as soon as possible to substantiate their belief that you can't succeed on your own.

What others think is of little consequence in determining *your* readiness to enter an intimate relationship and to enjoy fully the pleasures of your own healthy sexuality. Once you have dealt successfully with the anger and the guilt of your previous marriage, whether it ended through death or divorce, or of previous relationships if you have never married, then you will be ready to take a chance again. Every woman has to make her own choices, and the chapters that follow will help you in making the right choices in your life.

2

What's Your Pleasure?

"What do I want from romance?" laughs Susan, the divorced mother of two adolescents. "I want a sexy, funny, and intelligent man with a gorgeous body. He has to love to shoot baskets, fix bicycles, go to the opera, and eat meals at odd hours. Oh, yes, he must also leave me free to prepare briefs and to tend to the legal needs of corporate clients. He must be as successful as I hope to be, and he should also love children. And one more thing—he should not want to marry for a long while."

That description is a far cry from Susan's fantasy romance before she was married.

"If you had asked me what I wanted from romance when I was in college, I would have stopped with the first sentence," she says wryly. "Oh, how simple life was then. All I needed was a man who was attractive, fun, and intelligent. Children didn't come as part of the package then, and I had no thoughts of a career. Remember, I'm thirty-seven years old, and my traditional upbringing had me indoctrinated to believe that I would get an education, marry, work for a while, then have children and stay at home while my husband would support us in our little white home with the picket fence surrounding it. As Gomer Pyle used to say, 'Surprise, surprise.'

"After deciding that a wife and children were limiting his freedom, my husband sued for divorce. He then moved from our home in New Jersey to Texas after the divorce and left no forwarding address and, of course, no support. No, let me rephrase that. I could obtain his address if I wanted, but I'm glad to be rid of the disruptions. So five years later, I am now a lawyer, the kids are five years older, and we are going to buy that white house with the picket fence in a few months. Life has changed drastically, and what I want from romance also has to be different."

Deciding What You Want

Friend? Lover? Husband? A daddy for your children? Are you looking for a husband or just unmarried companionship? Should your children be involved, or do you want an "adults only" relationship?

"Any relationship that you have as a single mother, as long as it is energizing, will be good for your children," says Dr. Goodman. "When you date different men, even if it is only for a brief time, your children can benefit greatly if you have chosen wisely. Just meeting one more person who might tell them or show them something new in life is good for a child. Naturally, the men in your life should be selected carefully for your own sake as well as for the sake of your children. Men who will either ignore or mistreat your children will probably be indifferent to your needs, and they can be damaging to both you and your children."

You really have to take your total family situation into account, as well as your needs and preferences, when you consider romance. Although your likes and dislikes in a man may differ little from your taste before you had children, the presence of your child will make a big difference in how you relate to men.

Not every man who would have been right for you before you had children will be right for you now. If you are a widow, your needs will be different from those of a divorced or never-married mother. The ages of your children will also make a difference in how you handle a romantic relationship. Grown children present a different challenge from toddlers or adolescents.

Even if the relationship will take place largely outside of your home, the impact of the relationship on you will certainly influence your relationship with your children. A happy and fulfilled woman carries her satisfaction with life over into other areas, and children benefit from her happiness. On the other hand, a woman who is involved in a stormy love affair will have difficulty trying to hide her upset from her children.

As Dr. Victor Solomon emphasizes, "Your children are integral to your life, and they help to form the rhythms of your daily existence by their very being. That's why you must consider your children, and the nature of your life's rhythms, as you decide what you want from romance."

Love just "happens" for many of us, but love also dies quickly when there is no common basis upon which to build a romantic relationship. While you should not consider *only* your children when deciding on the type of man and the type of relationship that you want, your children should be an important element in making your choices.

Choices? Does the use of the word surprise you because you have often read that all the good men are either married, gay, or incarcerated?

Have you gotten tired of reading that the older a woman becomes, the lower her chances for remarriage?

Do your married friends bombard you with horror stories of those two out of three remarriages that fail?

In short, have you pretty much resolved that you will be lucky to find any eligible man, let alone be given the chance to make a choice regarding the who, what, when, and where of a romantic relationship?

Relax. There are many available men out there, although a good many of them may not be right for you. We'll be talking later in this book about the men who are available, and why certain types might be better for you than others.

Cold-blooded as it may seem, you should have a strategy before you actively seek to begin a romantic relationship. You should be selective, and you can afford to be selective if you decide in advance just what type of romantic relationship you want and what you can accommodate in your life.

It may be fun to fantasize about jetting about with a successful executive whose job takes him to a range of exotic destinations, but could you handle a romance with this man if he walked into your life today? Are your child-care arrangements so secure that you could pack a bag, kiss the kids good-bye, and meet your lover in an hour—for three weeks in Pago Pago? If not, then he's one option that you'll have to cross off your list of possibilities (even if such a choice is not even a remote possibility).

Could you, would you, leave your children with a caretaker for three weeks for any man? If not, then cancel the whole possible arrangement and decide to veto any romantic relationship with a man who expects you to travel with him on the spur of the moment.

Let's be a little more practical in examining your romantic possibilities. Although many divorced and widowed mothers want to remarry, many may not. That is the first decision that you should make before you begin to scout out the possibilities. Some men are for marrying, while other men are for enjoying without a license. The long-term commitment to marriage is substantially different from the decision to have a sexual relationship with a man. As Dr. Weiss cautions, you have to be careful that your sexual feelings do not fool you into believing that you are in love and ready to spend eternity together. Sex alone can be enough, as long as both you and your partner know that this is the situation. If the decision is one sided, then one of you will emerge bruised and shaken from what could be a satisfying and fulfilling relationship.

What Are Your Choices?

A world of possibilities is open to you, if you will only be flexible in considering your options. You can choose to seek out romance in a long-term relationship that will be exclusive or in a relationship that will lead to marriage.

On the other hand, if your goal is sexual satisfaction and you have no aim of marriage, you may be more interested in a series of short affairs, simultaneous relationships, or the infamous one-night stand, which may not be so infamous after all.

Before we look at each of these options, take some time to consider what the consequences of each arrangement may be for you and for your children.

Most professionals agree that single mothers who will involve their children in their relationships should consider long-term rather than short-term arrangements.

"Long-term relationships help to strengthen and to deepen feelings and they are better," points out Dr. Goodman, "but they are not fully necessary. Loving another human being is very healing to the body, to the emotions, and to the thinking process. Therefore, as long as you feel good about yourself and about your relationships, your children will have a similarly positive view."

Other professionals take a stronger stand regarding sex in the home. Dr. Marge Steinfeld, whose expertise is working with adolescents, advises strongly that single mothers aim for committed relationships if their children are to be aware of the mother's dating.

"If you want to have a number of men in your life, then it's better to keep them out of the sight of your children," she cautions. "Having one man after another in the house sets a standard for children, who are very impressionable. The example set by your behavior is what you will see in your own children as they grow older. For younger children, seeing a constant stream of men enter, then leave, their mother's life and their lives is disturbing. They become afraid to strike up any intimacy with others because no one seems to be around long enough."

Clinical psychologist Dr. Victor Solomon also recommends caution regarding the number and diversity of relationships.

"You have to stop and remember that your children will learn from what they see you doing," he notes. "You may feel that a series of one-night stands and numerous 'uncles' in the house are fine as long as your children don't actually catch you in the sex act. However, your children understand more than you know. Try as you may, your children will see your parade of men for what it is, and they will learn to behave in the same manner. You should not go out for a series of lovers if you believe that your child should at least be given a chance at a moral life and not have this determined for him by your behavior."

This doesn't mean that you must only aim for marriage as you begin seeking out romance. Rather, you have to consider the repercussions that who you date, where you meet, when you make love, and how often you go out will have on your relationship with your children and on their development.

Sex is a mystery to children, and they interpret what they see and hear in their own special way. This way is often very different from the way in which adults see the world, and it can lead to misunderstandings that carry throughout life. Sex is a topic fraught with the potential for misunderstanding.

Because it is such an awkward area for many Americans, not merely for single mothers, parents have found it difficult to speak about it with their children. As Dr. Goodman has observed, this is compounded by the fact that children at all ages tend to have false ideas about sex, and they may, especially, misinterpret what they observe about their mother's activities. While you should not advertise your sexual activities, neither should you be ashamed or embarrassed about your relationships.

One-Night Stands

"I'd have the kids stay with my sister," recalls forty-three-year-old Dina, "and I'd bring home anyone who interested me every Friday night for a year after my husband left. I didn't want to see any one man regularly. All I wanted was the feeling of a warm body next to me who made me feel desirable and attractive. I was so devastated when my seemingly steady and stable husband left me for a twenty-two-year-old punk-haired sales clerk that I went to bed with nearly any man who looked at me on those Friday nights. I hope that my kids never find out about that part of my life, because I'm not proud of it.

"I worked really hard to keep them from knowing what Mommy really did on those Friday nights, but I slipped up one night. Renny was four years old, and she awakened at three in the morning with a pain in her side. Instead of going into my sister's room to tell her, Renny slipped into the living room and dialed our number to tell me. Well, a little too much wine and some sexual athletics had put me into a deep sleep and I didn't hear the phone. But my 'guest' did, and he answered it. When I got on the line, Renny was crying and begging me to tell her who the stranger was in our apartment at three in the morning. She became hysterical and screamed for my sister to take her home right away. I had to get dressed and drive across town to pick the kids up.

"That experience was one of the last few one-night stands that I dared. Funny, the threat of AIDS, herpes, and murderers didn't have the sobering effect that hearing my daughter cry had on me. When I look back on those Friday nights, I shiver. They served a purpose, but I would never want my daughter to do the same!"

Not all single mothers take such pains to shield their children from their activities, in spite of warnings from psychology professionals that frequent, different lovers can adversely affect the development of the child. As Dr. Solomon has discovered from working with children in his practice, the youngest of children will be aware of sexual activity even when doors are securely locked.

"They hear noises, such as moans of pleasure and groans and the bedsprings squeaking," he states, "and they think that someone is being hurt in that locked room. When their mother brings in different somebodies and the same sounds are heard each time, then the child becomes very confused. He can only conclude that Mommy is hurt by the many men and that she must like being hurt because she brings men into her house. This may not only confuse the child in relation to how sex and intimacy are perceived, but it can affect the child's perception of all relationships between men and women."

Do one-night stands have a role in the life of the single mother? Women like Amy, thirty-four years old and the mother of four-year-old twins, claim that the one-night stand is their only option in certain age categories.

"Let's face it," she says in a resigned tone of voice. "I'm in the no-options age category. Most of the men near my age are still married with little children, or they're gay. Men in their forties are just breaking loose of their marriages and they want to swing, not play surrogate daddy to my children; and I don't find younger men attractive. I have a healthy appetite for sex, so I take whatever offers I receive. The offers that I receive are mainly for one-night encounters that end with men telling me that they will call. They never do call, and I no longer expect that they will.

"I'm very careful that the twins never meet any of the men, and I've worked out a very good plan. When I come home, I ask the man to wait in the car until I have paid the baby-sitter and sent her home. Then I check to make sure that the kids are soundly asleep before I go to the window and motion for the man to come up. We go quietly into the bedroom, and I make sure that I lock the door. I set the alarm on 'soft ring' for 4 A.M. and make sure that my 'date' gets up and out at that time. I have never been caught yet, and my children have never said anything to make me believe that they know about the men.''

Amy has been lucky, and not only because her children haven't awakened as she smuggles yet another stranger into their apartment. The reason that she has fallen into the rut of one-night stands is because she deliberately places herself into situations in which she meets men who are only looking for quick and easily forgotten sex.

With so many ways in which to meet men who might want more than a quick hop into her bed then out before daylight, Amy chooses to frequent a series of "pick-up" bars. While an occasional man or woman may meet someone special and establish a long-term relationship in this way, most of the patrons of these bars are just on the prowl. When she is confronted by the suggestion that she is choosing the bars in order to avoid finding men who can make a real commitment, Amy denies this vehemently. She refuses to admit that she is actually sabotaging her chances for meeting and getting to know men who would be open to more than one-night sex.

"Look, there are too many games to play at parties and when you meet somebody at work," she protests. "I know the score, and I know that there are more than enough women to go around. Why should I waste my time in trying to engage a man in conversation and in being pleasant and attentive company when he may just turn around and leave with someone who is five years younger and five points more attractive than me? At least at the bars we're all honest about why we're there."

Is she being realistic? Or is it more the case that Amy views herself as unable to sustain a relationship with a man? She is currently very successful at filling her bed whenever she desires to, but that sexual merry-go-round will slow down as time wears on.

Her children are also growing older, and Amy will not be able to count on them to sleep through her attempts to smuggle in men, nor to remain asleep throughout the night. She may find that her sexual adventures will be interrupted by frightened children who will awaken to the strange sounds coming from her bedroom, or her children may see her shepherding yet another "date" out the door. Such encounters may come sooner than she expects.

Not only has Amy been lucky because her children haven't discovered her adventures, she has also been spared the tragedies that can occur when strangers are welcomed into your home while your children sleep. Robbers, mutilators, and murderers can be charming individuals whose major asset can be their pleasant manner and their smile. A single mother who makes a habit of meeting and bedding strange men is playing the odds that she will not pick up a psychopath some evening. She is chancing that she will not bring home a mutilator. She is gambling that she and her children will not be the next victims of a disturbed person who preys upon unsuspecting women and children.

Is the preceding too melodramatic for your taste? Reconsider the possibilities before you brush away all concern.

AIDS and herpes, among the other antisocial "social" diseases, should also be thought of when you indulge in frequent and indiscriminate one-night sexual encounters. You may prefer to put such concern out of your mind and protest that only "other people" contract such diseases, but you may be unpleasantly surprised.

Cases of AIDS in women are being reported with increasing frequency because not every woman can be sure that the man with whom she is having nearly anonymous sex is not in one of the groups at risk. He may be bisexual, he may have been or may be an intravenous drug user, or he may have had sex with a prostitute who had AIDS. Can you afford to take the risk? As a single mother, do you have the right to take that risk?

Short Affairs

"How long is a 'short affair' to me?" asks Marcee, a widow with one son. "Oh, I don't know. Maybe three or four dates, or up to two months or so of being with each other. The point is that a short affair is just that—an affair. Neither the man nor I want it to go beyond just enjoying each other for a while. We never talk about next month, because there will probably be no next month. I never introduce my children, and I never meet his if he has any. In this way, nobody gets hurt. The beauty of such affairs is that, most of the time anyway, I can go to the man's place for sex. We get together enough to plan our encounters.

Of course, when I've had affairs with married men, we end up in a motel.''

Very much like the women who opt for only one-night stands, women like Marcee, who choose sexual arrangements that are apart from—and not a part of—their lives, do not seem to want to become emotionally involved with their partners.

"If I want to tell someone my troubles, I'll call my mother," says Marcee. "When I am with a lover, I don't want to hear about his problems with his job or with his life in general. That's why I have chosen to have brief affairs with several men rather than to become involved to the point that a man feels that he can pour his troubles out to me. He can't. I have my child and my own life, and my lovers are not a part of that life. That's the way that I want it for now. So why shouldn't I have it that way?''

Many single mothers prefer this detached approach to sex during the early days after the death of their husbands or after divorce. They view such detachment as a shield against getting hurt again if the partner leaves because they remain emotionally uninvolved. Although the one-night stands or short affairs may offer proof to a woman that she is still attractive and desirable, they lack any substance and offer little beyond sex. No shared intimacies, no emotional involvement, no continuity.

"I'll admit that I would like to have someone call me when I'm out of work with a cold," offers Marcee. "I'd be lying if I said that I don't miss having a man join my son and me at his birthday celebrations and other events. But the man who will be that involved will want a lot from me that I am not willing to give right now. Still, I have sexual needs and the need to be held in a man's arms. So until I'm ready to open my home and risk my son's happiness, I'm going to continue having brief affairs. No one gets hurt that way.''

No one gets hurt that way, but there is little emotional satisfaction for Marcee and none for her son. Furthermore, although Marcee's approach to meeting men is safer than those of the woman whose goal is the one-night stand, and she can more safely avoid men who may be dangerous, Marcee never allows herself to become too familiar with any of her lovers. As a result, she never knows whether or not any of her many lovers might pass AIDS, herpes, or anything else on to her. She won't risk becoming intimate enough with them to ask.

Single mothers such as Marcee, who engage in frequent brief affairs outside of the home, do not add anything to their children's lives, but that may be healthier than situations in which a single mother brings her numerous lovers home for her children to meet. In the attempt to be honest with her child, such a mother forces unwanted knowledge upon a child who may be confused by the appearance of a man who later disappears, only to be replaced by still another man.

Psychologists observe that a child who is placed in this position may come to feel that there is little permanence in life. As a result, he or she may develop an inability to make emotional attachments. They also caution against the habit of many single mothers to ask their children to call the different lovers "Uncle." As each "uncle" is replaced by still another, children learn, albeit subconsciously, that even relatives are not permanent. Nor can they trust their mother for very long as each new "uncle" is unceremoniously dropped and replaced by another.

Brief affairs may appear to offer a handy answer to meeting your sexual needs while not entangling your life in a relationship that will cause difficulty later. Nonetheless, they are not without complications. When you keep your affairs hidden from your children, you will probably have to make up excuses for your absences and keep your stories straight.

In addition, despite your intentions to remain emotionally distant, you will be emotionally affected by the beginning or the end of an affair and by its progress. Your children will sense your changing moods and, if there are no visible explanations for your mood shifts, they may well blame themselves and agonize over their part in such change.

On the other hand, if you choose to conduct your affairs in your home, your children may become attached to your lovers, however brief the affair. When the affair ends, you will have to help your child mourn the leaving of a man who was nothing more than a sexual partner to you. To your child, however, he may have been an "uncle" or a potential daddy, even if you did nothing to encourage the latter perception.

Conducted in either way, the short affair appears to have a greater impact on the life of the single mother and her children than might at first be evident. Although you may protest that you can remain emotionally detached, this may not be the uncomplicated route to a relationship that you wish it to be.

Long-Term and Committed

"I can't be morally neutral, in spite of my experiences as both a behavioral scientist and a social scientist," asserts psychologist Dr. Solomon. "I believe personally that marriage is the ideal relationship when children are involved. Professionally, however, my feeling is that if a single mother can't or won't marry, then she should refrain from having a series of lovers and instead establish a relationship with one person. Children learn by watching their mothers because mothers are also teachers. The most powerful school in the world is the home, and the most powerful teacher is the mother. Where there is no father, she is the only teacher."

This viewpoint may appear to be out of step with a society that advocates the development of a woman's potential and an expansion of the inner self. Furthermore, the emphasis upon commitment would appear to fly in the face of the movement of the last few decades away from dictating morality to individuals and toward "doing your own thing." When the well-being of children is the issue, however, psychologists tend to agree that a single mother must place a premium on considering the effect that her actions will have on the development of her children.

"A committed relationship is safer and more secure than a series of short affairs," observes Dr. Marge Steinfeld. "It is better for the child to have consistency in his life, if at all possible. This doesn't mean that the single mother has to marry. Rather, if her children are to be involved and for the relationship to be most satisfying, she should aim for a total relationship which includes the children."

A long-term relationship can take several forms, only one of which is marriage. Although some single mothers find that having a man move in with them and their children offers a workable arrangement, others vehemently oppose such arrangements.

"I agreed to date only Bill, and we soon found ourselves moving back and forth between our homes with kids, pets, and belongings," laughs Renee, a widowed mother of three children. "My children found our minimoves to be a blast. On some Saturdays, we packed up the car and went to Bill's for the whole day, while on other Saturdays, Bill came here with his two sons.

"Whenever Bill and I went out on a date alone, we would end up at one home or the other, and the kids had strict orders to knock before entering our respective bedrooms. They're all in the age range of nine through thirteen, so we could make that point quite clearly. Because of the kids, however, we haven't spent the night together, and I don't really miss that.

"One evening when I mentioned it, Bill told me that he was happy with that restriction, too, because he likes having the whole bed to himself, and he also likes waking up by himself and not having to immediately turn on the charm. The kids are also content with having Bill and his kids around sometimes, but not all the time. In some ways, I'd say that I have the best of both worlds. I have a secure relationship with Bill, we have our families, and we also have our own surroundings. We'll see where we go in the future."

The casual yet committed relationship that Renee enjoys with Bill allows them to have each other while continuing to live their own lives within their own surroundings. There appears to be no pressure to formalize the commitment, and they are both wise enough to realize that combining their families into one home could cause complications that neither desires at this point. Their amiable relationship might carry over into a living-together arrangement, but the mere issue of space can be enough to make them regret a move.

While single mothers such as Renee are highly satisfied with a committed relationship in which the partners live apart, many others prefer to have a relationship in which both partners share the same home.

"How could we say that we had made a commitment if we were commuting between homes?" questions Deirdre, the thirty-seven-year-old divorced mother of a boy, six, and a girl, eight. "To me, making a commitment means that you come as close to marriage as possible without actually being married. I would have preferred marriage. However, Jeff was really hurt in his divorce, and he's afraid to try again. So we agreed to live together for a while. My children had gotten to know Jeff very well over the four months that we dated before he moved in. We had dinner together, went boating, visited the zoo and parks, and built up some memories. After the first two months, they would ask about him if he wasn't here every evening. When I finally had him stay the night, my children saw it as a natural act, and no one questioned his presence at breakfast. That's when we began talking about living together. After mentioning it to the kids, I realized that they were all for it."

Deirdre seems to be happy with the arrangement, even though she would prefer to be married to Jeff. The children are also content with the arrangement because Jeff is not just their mother's lover. Instead, he has become part of the total relationship of the family. There has only been one incident to mar their happiness, and that occurred at the children's school.

Jeff usually picked the children up whenever Deirdre couldn't get out of work on time, and everyone seemed to assume that he was their father. One afternoon, Deirdre's son told Jeff that his teacher wanted to see his mother immediately. Since Deirdre wasn't there, Jeff decided to fill in.

When they walked into the classroom, the teacher smiled brightly and said, "Oh, Sam, I'm glad that you brought your father right up with you."

To which Sam replied, equally brightly, "Oh, no. This isn't my father. This is my mother's boyfriend, Jeff. He lives with us!"

The teacher made a quicker recovery from that remark than did Jeff, who later vowed never to pick up the kids from school again.

There is one other type of relationship for which you may aim as a single mother—marriage. As you already know, not only is marriage the longest term of the long-term relationships, but it also requires the most intense commitment of all relationships that you might seek. This option will be discussed in greater detail in a later chapter.

As a divorced, widowed, or never-married mother, you may have serious reservations about marriage as a goal for a relationship. Still, it is an option that you should consider as you determine the type of relationship that you want. Knowing what you want will enable you to become involved in the right situations and to meet the right men who will help you achieve your goals for a romantic relationship, whatever they may be.

Before considering the men who are available and where to meet them, take the time to consider how your status of being divorced, widowed, or never-married significantly affects your options and influences your willingness to become involved with certain types of men in specific types of relationships.

3

Is There Life After Divorce?

"In some ways it's a shame that I wasn't widowed instead of divorced," Shana observes with a bitter edge to her voice. "Of course, my son is content with his relationship with his father, and the financial support does help. Still, even with all of the divorced women in this country, overcoming the image problem and the feelings of distrust are difficult. Just when you think that you can move about freely and raise your child as you please, society, your ex-husband and his family, and the old bugaboos about making the same mistake again jump out in front of you. I felt that I had to face up to a lot before I felt free to date again."

Few divorced mothers are as candid about their situations as Shana, although most appear to realize that they have a lot of old business to resolve before they can enjoy satisfactory romantic involvements.

A Fear of Trying

While a minority of divorced women ignore the comments and criticism of their families, their ex-husbands, and their children and begin dating frantically as soon as they or their husbands have moved out, most approach dating with trepidation.

If you have been hurt by marriage, you may want to stay away from men for a while. You may have negative feelings about marriage in general and about men in particular to resolve. In addition, if sex was a problem in your marriage, it will also be a source of insecurity to you when you begin to consider dating. Many women also carry a sense of guilt about the marriage, blaming themselves needlessly for its demise. Before any divorced woman can feel ready for a new romance, she will have to deal with these issues in her life.

For some divorced mothers, however, the anger and hurt of divorce may have another effect. Such women want to connect as soon as possible in order to "show" their ex-husbands and to prove to themselves that they are still physically desirable.

Whichever route you consider, unlike the widow or the never-married mother, you may have to deal with a variety of emotional issues that affect you and your children, both individually and jointly. As a divorced mother, you may find yourself faced with one or more of the following tasks before you can put aside the complexities of life and turn your attention to romance and sexual companionship. Among your new concerns may be the following:

- Adjusting to your new role
- Overcoming the feelings of rejection that emerge when a husband leaves
- Putting an unhappy and disappointing marriage into perspective
- Coping with the emotional and financial upsets that divorce creates for you and your children
- Negotiating support and custody issues with your ex-husband
- Steeling yourself against the criticism of an ex-husband and his family
- Trying to identify what went wrong in the effort to avoid future suffering

Divorced—Not a "Divorcée"

We may live in a sexually liberated society, but many divorced mothers who live outside of major metropolitan areas do not enjoy the anonymity that comes with life in a large city. The label "divorcée" still represents a certain stigma. In addition, many divorced mothers have found that the term may even imply a specific moral character and expected behavior among certain cultural and ethnic groups.

If you live in an ethnically homogeneous neighborhood, or if you retain strong family ties, this will come as no surprise to you.

Even outside of ethnic enclaves, women have found that society still views the divorced mother in a different—and often harsher—light than other single women.

"I remember when my mother divorced my father twenty-five years ago," recalls Maria, thirty-three, the divorced mother of two girls. "Her large Italian family expected her to feel like a failure and to somehow 'pay' for being divorced. It may seem strange now, but the men that she met, and even those that she had worked with for years, assumed that she was sexually available because she was this 'hot number'—a *divorcée*. My mother, a hot number!

"I was only ten years old when I first heard some of the boys in my class talking about her, and I thought that the kids were talking about somebody else. She was positively prim and proper by today's standards. I think of that when I am tempted to accept a date with someone who teaches where I do, or when I am asked out by a man who has just learned that I'm divorced. That's part of the reason that I have refused a lot of dates."

The divorced single mother today is less likely to be viewed in so exotic a light as her counterpart of two or three decades ago because sheer numbers have made her a more familiar figure. Still, even better-educated divorced mothers tend to view their lives as being lived under constant scrutiny by their family, their friends, their children, and their children's school.

"I watch what I say about my social life, and I'm very careful in how I dress," says one young divorced mother. "I'm only twenty-six years old and have a pretty good figure, in spite of having had three children in four years. Because I'm afraid that the men where I work will get the wrong idea, I wear more tailored styles and darker colors to work than the married women. I'm even afraid to join in the light flirting with the married executives for fear that they will think that I am 'easy.'

"You may think that this is ridiculous in 1986, but I need this job and the solid executive training that comes with it. I've already seen one divorced single mother drummed out of the company because the 'old boy network' mistook her friendly banter for sexual come-ons. My social life can wait until I am secure in a career."

You may not have experienced such overt reminders of the distant past—and sometimes present—in which the "divorcée" was pictured as an exotic and sensual creature who promised easy sex with no attachments. For a better reminder, take a look at the late-night movies of the last two decades.

The images of divorced women with children have been a little better, but the stigma persists in some quarters. You may also perceive this stigma, even if you can't cite specific incidents.

Take a moment to consider your own reaction to the label "divorcée." Many women choose to avoid this term in describing their marital status because of the numerous unfavorable associations. They prefer instead to refer to themselves as "divorced mothers." The difference on paper is minimal, but the difference in meaning is great.

Sex and the Divorced Mother

The immediate reaction of many women who have been left by their husbands for another woman—or for any other reason—is to go out and attract and bed as many men as they can in as a short a space of time as possible. Feeling desirable, if only for an hour or so, helps to combat the fears and doubts that a woman feels when her husband has literally told her that she is no longer worthy of his love. Although this period of frenzied dating may provide a temporary satisfaction, most women find that it can have long-term catastrophic effects on later attempts to date and to successfully negotiate their lives.

How then can you satisfy your romantic and sexual needs and rebuild your damaged ego while maintaining an acceptably "respectable" image? Your first step should be to realize that a sexual binge that requires seducing all available men simply to acquire notches on your bedboard is a frantic gesture that will have very much the same results as an eating binge. After you have been sated, and after you have had the time to examine your actions, you will most likely be upset with the wasted effort and the aftereffects. Of course, the aftereffects of an indiscriminate sexual binge can be more serious to both your emotional health and your physical health than might an indiscriminate eating binge.

Rather than making you feel sexy, desirable, and worthy, a sexual binge of one-nighters will probably leave you feeling tired, empty, and wasted.

If you have been really indiscriminate in your sexual partners, you may have the additional—and not insignificant—problems of having acquired one or more "social" diseases such as herpes or gonorrhea, or even the more devastating AIDS (acquired immune deficiency syndrome) if your partners have included bisexual men, intravenous drug users, or men who may have frequented prostitutes.

Should you have been careless with your chosen form of birth control—and you may have been if you were feeling reckless—you may even have to deal with a pregnancy that will further complicate your life by forcing more choices on you. Will you have the child—or an abortion? Either way, how will the man be involved? Should he be involved?

The wages of sin? Hardly. These dire warnings are offered simply in an effort to remind you that you can do more damage to your ego and to your life in the long run if you believe that indiscriminate and frantic sex will restore your feelings of self-worth and self-esteem; you need to take a more conservative and, yes, an even more boring path to achieve this.

You have to have a healthy self-image if you are going to attract the kind of man who will love and cherish both you and your children.

Think about that for a moment. How have you viewed yourself in the past? You may have found that your feelings of self-worth, or lack of self-worth, were often mirrored in others' actions toward you. People, and particularly lovers, can value you only as highly as you value yourself. Thus, if you view yourself as worthless or insignificant, you are only inviting others to do the same.

When you project an image of healthy self-confidence, you are telling others that you know who you are and that you are a worthwhile and valuable individual. A husband who has left, a date who rejects you, children who test your patience, and friends and family who try to wear you down will be unable to shake your faith in yourself. Once you have developed a healthy self-esteem, there will be no need to prove your worth by carving notches on the bedboard. You can now begin to explore and enjoy true romantic involvement and satisfying sexual intimacy.

After you have nursed your ego back to health, however, you may be left with the problem of maintaining a "respectable" image for the rest of the world. This can be less of a problem than you may expect it to be. When you value yourself, you also find that you can live your own life with greater confidence.

The image that you project to the rest of the world should be an image that pleases you and not one that is designed to please everyone else. If your choice is to appear to be the solicitous mother who has no romantic involvements, then that is your choice. If you choose to project the image of a happily integrated personality who has learned to balance both motherhood and romance, then that is another choice. Should your image of choice be that of a sensuous and new woman, your secure self-esteem will permit you to project that image.

In short, "maintaining a 'respectable' image" is an open-ended goal that depends largely on your personal definition of what constitutes a "respectable" image. Secure self-esteem will give you the confidence to live out whatever image you conceive.

Free Yourself for Romance

Your former husband can be a strong influence on your success in both seeking out and nurturing intimate relationships. Not only do many divorced women find that they must exorcise the ghosts of the marriage and divorce before they can feel free to love again, but they must also deal with the interference of the former spouse in their current social lives. The divorce may sever the marriage, but you and your former husband will be forever bound together in the form of your memories and through your most valuable joint effort—your children.

If your divorce was messy, you may find that relaxing with a man and trusting him will be difficult. You may be consciously aware that your bad experience in marriage was only with one man, and that the same difficulties need not occur with another man. You may also admit freely to a share in the responsibility for the failure of the marriage.

Nonetheless, somewhere in the back of your mind and your heart will lurk the frightening suspicion that it could happen again. Such fear can be paralyzing, and may lead you to isolate yourself from all men in the hope of avoiding further emotional pain.

"I can't help but wonder if each new man I date is just going to be a carbon copy of my ex," muses Rita, thirty-six, the divorced mother of Rona, twelve, and Larry, fourteen. "I went out with one man who was just like Jim. He constantly interrupted me when I spoke, quibbled with the waiter over the check, and seemed to disagree with my opinion on everything. It's happened in varying degrees at other times, and I'm getting pretty gun-shy about dating. Let's face it—if all I'm going to find are reruns of my miserable marriage, I may as well enter a convent!"

Not all divorced mothers assume such attitudes of blame, but many do find that they are wary of romance or of any social contact with men. An unpleasant marriage and a difficult divorce may cause a divorced mother to withdraw from the company of men at least for a time. Such women can't shake the feeling that men are the enemy. They feel that they will only be hurt if they spend time with men.

Such behavior is damaging not only to you as a woman, but it can also be damaging to the self-image of your children, who should see you interact in a healthy manner with people of both sexes.

As difficult as it may be for you, rather than condemn all men because of one unpleasant situation, you owe it to yourself to confront your anger and your hurt. Neither men nor women are saints, nor are they natural enemies. Rather than isolating yourself from men and thus cheating yourself of the pleasures of romance and sexual intimacy, examine your reasons for your feelings. Once you know why you are hesitant to open your life to romance, you can learn how to overcome the obstacles to your happiness.

Use the following questions as a guide in identifying your reasons for hesitance:

1. What are your current feelings toward your former husband?
2. What kind of person were you in your former marriage as a wife, a mother, a lover, a partner?
3. In which of these roles did your husband find you to be most satisfying during the marriage? Least satisfying?
4. In which of these roles did you view yourself as being most satisfying during the marriage? Least satisfying?

5. Which of these roles would be important to the men that you might date?
6. How satisfied would they be with your fulfillment of the role(s)?
7. How accurate were your former husband's criticisms of your abilities, character, and appearance?
8. Have you changed since your marriage ended? If so, have any of the criticisms expressed by your former husband become invalid?
9. What did you like the most about yourself during your marriage? What did you like the least?
10. What do you like the most about yourself now? What do you like the least?

After answering the questions, take a careful look at the differences between your assessment of your behavior and abilities during your marriage and the way in which you view yourself now. During your marriage, did you view yourself mainly through your husband's perspective, however unfavorable it may have been? Do you still view yourself through his perspective? Are you convinced that the men you meet will also view you from that perspective? If that is your feeling, then you are wasting precious time by locking yourself in the past.

The man that you married is not *all* men. He doesn't represent the opinions of all men, and his actions are not the actions of all men. The fact that you interacted in one way with him does not mean that you will interact in the same way with other men that you meet. In addition, the men that you meet will not have the same opinion of you as your former husband, nor will they hold the same expectations for you.

Some of them might echo your former husband in specific ways, but many of them will not. To find those who are different, however, you will have to take a chance on romance. You may be a big winner.

Peeping-Tom Ex-Husbands

Men's reactions when their former wives begin to date vary as widely as the personalities of the men themselves. Some former husbands try to extract every detail of a woman's romantic relationships from their children during periods of visitation, with no further action. Other former husbands protest outright that their former wives have no right to romantic relationships and that implied sexual intimacy is morally harmful to their children. Still others physically threaten their former wives if they are even seen in public in the company of another man.

Such behavior is hardly unusual, and it is a sign of varying degrees of immaturity in men who want to maintain some claim on the lives of their former wives. Not all men are so possessive after a divorce, but many women do complain that their former spouses make getting romantically involved difficult.

"The kids are caught right in the middle, again," says forty-two-year-old Myrna, the mother of two sons. "They don't mind me going out on Friday nights, but they *hate* the game of 'Twenty Questions' that their father subjects them to each Sunday when he takes them to dinner. 'Who is your mother going out with?' 'How often does she go out?' 'How late does she come home?' They don't feel right if they answer his questions, but they don't want to tell him to stop because he may be angry with them. As for me, I just wish the marital cord could finally be cut."

A situation in which your every move is monitored can cramp your romantic style, and it lessens your assurance of sexual intimacy. How you cope with the ways in which a former spouse may sabotage your move toward romance and sexual intimacy depends strongly on the nature and attitude of his interference and on the nature of your present relationship with him.

If you are on relatively friendly terms, you may find that you can explain your feelings about his interest in your personal life and express your concern that the children are highly uncomfortable in the role of messenger. He may not even realize that what he may view as "conversation" with your children is taken as prying into your personal life.

Even if the possibility is uncomfortable, you have to be firm in making your point that you and your ex-husband are no longer married. You have the right to date, to fall in love, and, should you choose, to remarry. He has the same right.

Even if he does remarry, you may still be plagued by jealous possessiveness unless you resolve the issue at the onset. The problem is made more difficult if your former husband abused you physically during the marriage and if he continues to physically threaten you after the divorce. You may have to get a court order to protect yourself from his threats of harm. Consult your attorney for your own protection.

Life does not end with divorce. Rather, the end of your marriage can provide you with a new beginning in life and a new chance for you and your children to find happiness. You have the opportunity to put aside the old hurts and disappointments and to start fresh. You also have the opportunity to find new love.

Romance and sexual fulfillment are not just pleasures to be enjoyed by other women. They are also your right. But they are a right that you have to claim through your new belief in yourself and your willingness to take a chance again.

4

When Does the Mourning End?

"How can I be a *widow* when I'm only twenty-four years old and have a three-year-old son?" Geri asks her question with a sense of despair. "Widows are supposed to be older, with grown children, and with most of their life behind them. I feel like my life has been cut short. My son and I have been cheated!"

Facing widowhood is no easier for forty-two-year-old Anne, the mother of a teenager, or for sixty-seven-year-old Delia, whose three children are adults with their own families.

"Bob and I were just beginning to have the money to enjoy all the little luxuries that we couldn't afford when we were first married," explains Anne. "My son Tim is entering college this fall. Bob and I had giggled like two teenagers as we planned the wild and sexy nights that we would have once we would be alone. Now it will be only me, and I really am alone."

"I've always looked forward to the 'golden years' with Jim," Delia says sadly. "We made plans to travel, to sleep late, and to generally enjoy life at a slower pace than we had when we were both working. Jim had lost his grandparents when he was very young, and he very much wanted to be a good 'grandpa' to our grandchildren. Now . . ." Delia's voice fades as she tries to suppress a sob.

Widowed—But Still Alive

American women are not physically buried alive with their husbands, nor are they burned to ashes on a funeral pyre with their husbands, as widows have been in other cultures and in other civilizations. They suffer a different but equally terrible fate. All too often, family, friends, and children expect a widow to continue to revere the memory of her late husband and to limit her participation in life as a sign of her loyalty.

In many cases, a widow becomes a passive co-conspirator in her own emotional imprisonment. She will lock herself away from the outside world and even from her own children as she tries to keep from seeming disloyal in the least. Rather than reaching out for someone to fill the void left by her husband, a widow will hang on to his memory. This is not the case for widowers, whose periods of mourning are often significantly shorter than those of widows. In short, as one past president of the National Funeral Directors Association puts it, "Women grieve, but men remarry."

"I was invited to a party six months after Bob died," Anne recalls. "The hostess was a close friend whom I had avoided since Bob's death. The party was a chance for a rekindling of our friendship as well as my 'debut' from widowhood and back into the world. I agonized over the decision to go.

"My parents frowned when I told them, and reminded me that only six months had passed. Friends that had been close to Bob and me as a couple suggested with the hint of a leer that the hostess was probably trying to fix me up with a date. I would never have gone if Tim hadn't shaken me up by telling me that I had really let my life become a shambles."

Her son Tim, a tall, handsome eighteen-year-old college student, had looked Anne squarely in the eye and told her that she had been wallowing in her misery for six months.

"Maybe you *shouldn't* go to the party," Tim had told her. "You don't look very much like you did when Dad was alive. You don't use makeup anymore, your clothes are just thrown on, and your hair is just combed and pinned back. I think that the way you look is unfair to Dad's memory."

Anne had been deeply hurt by those words, but she was more hurt by the truth in them.

"Tim was right," she now says. "I would have been *ashamed* to let Bob see me in that condition. It hurt, but Tim's candidness shook me out of my misery. I went to the party, and I had a very good time. That was my debut into life once again."

If you have been widowed, then you probably have your own stories of how others tried to make you feel guilty if you looked too healthy, too happy, or too content with your new life as a woman alone.

- Your friends will ask how you are getting along without your husband, and you will hesitate to admit that you may be functioning quite well.
- Your family may suggest that you and your children move in with them, and you will hesitate to tell them that you like having your own life.
- Your children will glance at you with disapproval if you sing too happily or plan to go out, even with friends, too often. If you look like you are having fun in life, they will ask you, "Don't you miss Dad?"

Living Your Own Life

You have two choices when people try to make you feel guilty for enjoying life when your spouse has died: submit or resist.

Submitting to widowhood means becoming a social, psychological, and physical widow. Widows who submit to guilt deny themselves even the smallest pleasures that come their way. They may or may not take on the role of martyr, but their self-denial is evident nonetheless.

Parties are out. "How can I enjoy myself when all I can think of is Gary?"

Social relationships are out. "Don't they know that all I can think of is Gary?"

Romance and sex are out. "How can I ever love any man but Gary?"

Even living becomes "out." "Why couldn't I have died instead of Gary?"

Why would any woman punish herself in this way?

Women who feel this way may very likely be plagued by unresolved grief over the loss of their husbands. Such feelings are natural right after the death of a husband, but you should seek professional bereavement counseling if such feelings persist after six months.

"The widow has gone through genuine grief, and she may be dealing with guilt feelings for not having been a better wife, not loving him enough, not preventing his death, et cetera," states Dr. Victor Solomon, based on his experiences with widows in bereavement counseling. "Although she may feel good about marriage and about men, she may find that beginning a social life will be made difficult by these guilt feelings. A widow will also have difficulty in getting involved with another man, because a new involvement will seem like a betrayal of a marriage that was so happy or that seemed to be so happy. At the same time, the happiness of the marriage may make such involvement even more important to the widow than to either the divorced or never-married mother."

Many women tend to succumb to the disapproval and the expectations of family, friends, or children, who themselves may be in shock over the death.

"Jake's brothers told me at the funeral that I always had family to call on, instead of 'strangers,'" says Terry. "They implied, rather strongly, that I should have no need for socializing since the family unit was large, nor should I *need* to see other men because Jake had left me materially well provided for. The clincher was when they compared me to their mother, widowed in her early thirties with three sons to raise. She had kept their father's picture on the mantel and frequently referred to what he might think in various situations. I was also reminded that she never went out with another man after their father died. Since I, too, had children, they expected that I would also be the fine mother—widow—that their mother had been.

"I was flabbergasted. But do you want to know something? Although I inwardly boiled with rage, I *did* seclude myself in the first months. I clicked on the answering machine, didn't return calls, and didn't accept any invitations. The only people that I talked with were my children, my parents, and Jake's family.

"After a few months, the act of submitting to widowhood became a natural role for me. However, it also became boring to the very people who had advised me to assume that role. No one wanted to hear how much I missed Jake, nor did they care that I was 'true to his memory.' I was sick of it, so I threw out the black clothes and went shopping. After saying 'The hell with it,' I bought some bright clothes and took my kids out to dinner. It's just too bad that I wasted those months in playing a role to please others. I'm ready to live and to enjoy life."

Being a widow should not mean living a life in death. That doesn't mean that you should not revere the memory of your late husband; nor should you block out all references to the past. Your past and your children's past are the foundation upon which the present and the future are built. For your own sake and for the sake of your children, you have to create a new life that incorporates the past but which is not dominated by it.

Will you satisfy everyone, or even anyone, aside from yourself? Probably not. Then again, whose life is it? Your children need a living mother in addition to their memories of their late father. You deserve to live and to enjoy life while keeping your precious memories intact.

If you submit to the demands of others, then you will live the life that others choose for you. That is not truly living.

Resistance to the expectations of others who seem ready to create your image as a widow can be subtle. When friends meet you and accusingly tell you that you look very well, thank them for the compliment.

When family tells you that you should move in with them or that you should be more reclusive, thank them for their concern.

When your children tell you that you seem to be too happy and that you don't seem to miss their father, hold them and tell them how grateful all of you should feel to be together. They, most of all perhaps, have shared the deep loss with you. They have lost a father as you have lost a husband.

They, most of all, must be helped to understand that life and love must not stop with death but that loving someone who has died gives us the experience with living that should help us to live even richer and more love-filled lives.

Most of all, your children should be helped to understand that loving someone else is not a betrayal of their love or your love for their father. It is instead an affirmation of that love.

Sex and the Widowed Mother

You have to give yourself permission to love again before others will grant you that same right. Doing so, however, may not be easy. Deciding to have a sexual relationship will be vastly more difficult.

It has been said that however bad the marriage and the husband, they both improve greatly when a woman becomes a widow. Whether true or not, few widows will publicly admit to anything but a marriage that was one of continuous bliss, and a husband who was a saint or, at the very least, wonderful. Society considers it unseemly to say otherwise.

The often genuinely happy memories that widows hold of their marriages makes them more likely to want to remarry than women who have been divorced. As Dr. Victor Solomon has observed, "Widows have had happy experiences with marriage, or at least they believe that their experiences have been happy. As a result, they are more likely than the divorced woman to take a chance on marriage."

There is, however, a difference between showing respect for the memory of your late husband and committing the error of making him a man of saintly perfection. You should certainly help your children to retain the good memories of their father, but they should also be permitted to remember his flaws. He was human. To wipe out all reference to his less-than-perfect actions and characteristics is to create a false god that will demand not only your worship but your servitude.

Once you have created a god from the memory of your husband, how can any other man hope to meet your expectations or those of your children? How could any man be considered even adequate as a mate?

Others will be more than willing to deny you permission to begin a social life. Young children will cling to you as a means of holding on to some part of their old life in which their father played a part. They may also be very frightened that they will lose you as they have lost their father. You will have to slowly prepare them for your dating, and reassure them that you love them now and that you will continue to love them and be with them.

Older children will view your attempts at a social life with jealousy that even they might not recognize. The adolescent son, who is experiencing his own bodily changes and a new sexual awareness, doesn't want to think that his mother is romantically involved with a man. Not only does he view this as a betrayal of his father, but he sees her dating as a betrayal of him.

Sons frequently assume a protective role toward their mothers when the father dies. A woman may try to discourage such feelings, but they emerge nonetheless. Daughters, on the other hand, view a dating mother as competition, and they may resent a mother who has an active social life.

Added to these normal adolescent difficulties is the memory of the father, which must be respected but which must not be allowed to overshadow your present. Even when children are adults with families of their own, a mother who has been widowed will face resistance to her social life. Older children have had a longer life as children of both parents. As a result, they are often even more opinionated and judgmental about their mother's life.

How can a widow have a successful romantic life without upsetting her children?

"Discretion is the key," points out Dr. Steinfeld. "Don't talk a lot about your dating, but don't hide it, either. Instead, make it clear to your children that you love them very much and that your social life enhances your life but that it does not negatively affect your life with them."

Widowed mothers, more than divorced or never-married mothers, have greater difficulty in choosing to have a sexual relationship that is not headed for marriage. While the divorced mother may, after some time, lead a man home and to her bed, the widowed mother must contend not only with the normal need for discretion with her children, but she and her lover may very well be heading for her marital bed.

Until they are faced with a lover in their bedrooms, many women do not think about the implications of this scenario.

"I was disgusted by myself," recalls Alice, a forty-two-year-old widow. "My children were away at camp, and the home was all ours. I had finally decided that I was ready to have a steamy and passionate affair with a man whose touch made me shiver. We had dinner and returned to my home for a nightcap and for wonderful lovemaking. I deserved to enjoy Len. It had been so long since I had felt the weight of a man's body on me or the pure pleasure of sex without promises or regrets. It all went beautifully until we walked into the bedroom, our arms wrapped around each other, caressing each other and aching to throw our clothes off and make love. Then I saw that bed. My husband and I had slept in that bed for sixteen years. For chrissake, we had picked out the bed together and grinned slyly while the salesman wrote out the bill. How could I dare to bring another man into that bed? Our bed?

"I ran back to the living room and poured a drink, spilling it on myself as I sobbed. I was so ashamed of what I had almost done, and I was angry, too. Angry for being a widow. Angry at the bed. Angry at myself. Len didn't understand what had happened, and he left right away. I explained the next day when he called, and he told me to 'get back to him' when I had 'worked it out.' I guess that he wasn't worth it anyway, but he served a purpose. He forced me to realize that I had to unload the past if I wanted to start loving and enjoying life again.

"I had the bed taken away and bought a new queen-sized bed that is all my own. My children were a little surprised, but they accepted my explanation that having the old bed made me too sad. That was very close to the truth."

Even when you don't bring men home, your past may very much affect your sexual present. Old ways of making love, your favorite positions, or old familiar ways of touching may intrude upon your present relationship. You may use these remembrances of things past as an excuse for declaring the new man in your life to be an inadequate lover. In this way, you can safely view him as being inferior to your late husband and not worth your time.

On the other hand, if your new man satisfies you sexually and romantically, you may also make the mistake of ending the relationship due to the nagging fear of being unfaithful to a memory—that of your late marriage. Either way, you are cheating yourself. No man will ever be your late husband. No man can have all of his good points—or all of his bad points. Be realistic and accept the fact that no man should have to be only a carbon copy of one who has died.

More important, you are a different person today from who you were when you were married, and you deserve the right to explore and to attain sexual pleasure with anyone you choose.

The Men in Your Life

"There is no area in which her late husband wasn't smarter, more skilled, or just plain better than me," complains forty-five-year-old Darren, who is dating a forty-three-year-old widow with three children. "And the kids aren't any better. I feel as if I am constantly being compared to this superhuman who was superdad, superhusband, and superman all rolled up into one body!"

Few men can compete with the legendary late husband and feel adequate, but their fears of inadequacy are often unfounded. While you and your children may play a large part in creating the memory of the superhuman father that we spoke of earlier, you must realize that many men also enter a relationship with the fear of measuring up to your late husband.

You don't have to lie or deliberately downgrade your late husband's memory to make the men you meet more comfortable. Instead, you should be honest with them, but first be honest with yourself.

Did Brad really drive better than the man that you've begun dating? Or does it just seem that way?

Was Brad really more good-looking and virile than the man that you've begun dating? Or do you just remember him that way?

Was Brad really more cultured than the man you are now dating? Or did he just give the impression that he was?

More important, ask yourself why you loved Brad. Was it because he was a good driver, good-looking, virile, and well-educated? Most women would shake their heads to that question, because love doesn't grow out of such surface concerns. Why then does your present man have to compete with the memory of surface concerns? Why is it necessary for you and your children to keep reminding your new man, however subtle the hints, that Brad was better in every way?

The truth may be that you don't feel that he is good enough to take your late husband's place. The need to have someone, *anyone*, may be keeping you together, even if you view him as being inferior to the sort of man that you can truly love.

That charge may seem to be harsh, but it is often true. If it weren't, then why would a woman date someone who clearly doesn't meet her standards? And if a man is constantly told that he fails in this, that, or another category, he can hardly be said to be adequate.

Of course, most widows and their children do not consciously downgrade the men in their lives. They do so as a way to somehow tell everyone else that they are remaining loyal to their late father's or husband's memory.

It is not because of your desire to hurt the new man that you are dating that pictures of your late husband remain prominently displayed, or that the abilities and talents of your late husband are compared with those of the new man. Instead, you may have a subconscious need to produce tangible evidence, in the form of the pictures, and emotional reassurance, through reminders of the qualities of your past husband, that you have not forgotten him or abandoned his memory.

Your children may also need such evidence to help them to overcome the guilt that they feel in enjoying your new companions. With the pictures and the references to the superiority of their late father, they can safely absolve themselves of the perceived crime of disloyalty.

The happiness of your former marriage may lead you to feel that no one can ever take your late husband's place. No one can. No one should. Instead, there is room for more happiness and for more love in your life, to add to what you already hold in your memory. Finding someone whom you can love may take a while, and it probably will because the loss was great. As you may find, widowed mothers often take the longest time to begin dating because their loss is greater than that of either the divorced or the never-married mother.

Furthermore, because the death often comes abruptly, you may be left with a great deal of anger to overcome, in addition to your deep feelings of grief. You may need to obtain qualified therapy to aid you in dealing with your anger and grief if you find that they are keeping you from rejoining the rest of the world and if they are preventing you from living the life of love that you deserve.

You have a life of your own to live, to lead, and to enjoy. Becoming a widow did not lower your capacity to love or your need to be loved; neither did it eliminate your capacity to enjoy sensual and sexual pleasure. These remain within you, waiting to be invited out again when the right man comes along at the right time. In the meantime, you can make yourself ready.

5

What's Wrong With Being Never-Married?

"When I had Steven, eighteen years ago," recalls Marion, "the terms 'illegitimate' and 'unwed mother' were still in vogue. I was financially independent and working in a high-prestige position with a well-known magazine. Although people close to me advised me to have an abortion, there was never any pressure placed on me by the publisher, nor did I suffer professionally. That's one of the marvelous aspects of being in the creative world."

The well-dressed and attractive fifty-four-year-old woman pauses, pondering her next words. She is a woman in control who seems to have always been in control of her life. Having a child without fulfilling society's demand that she marry was a risky venture eighteen years ago, but the decision was carefully considered and wisely made. Today, Marion seems satisfied with the way in which she has directed her life.

Not every never-married mother chooses to become pregnant, as many of you may know from firsthand experience. Even in today's relaxed social atmosphere, many women remain uncomfortable in telling others that they never did marry their baby's father. Sociologists have observed that the stigma is less prominent within many lower socioeconomic subgroups, in which the frequency of never-married childbearing has become a norm. However, as Dr. Steinfeld points out, for the majority of never-married mothers, admitting to having chosen a child but not a husband is uncomfortable.

Neither "Unwed" Nor "Illegitimate"

"There's something very negative about the terms 'unwed' and 'illegitimate,' " Ruth states firmly as she pokes the air with her finger. "People seem to be so judgmental in declaring me not married and in labeling my daughter not legitimate. I'm glad that Diane was born in a time when 'illegitimate' wasn't put on her birth certificate. It's a nasty word."

Ruth, now twenty-six, was seventeen when she became pregnant with Diane. A high school senior, she had fought the demands of her parents and her boyfriend that she obtain an abortion and go on with her life. She was in no position to have a child, and she had really tried not to become pregnant. Still, by the middle of her senior year, her stomach looked as if she were wearing a small pillow under her pullover sweaters.

"I am a mother, and not very different from a divorced mother whose ex-husband is mainly absent, except that we don't have the hassles of visitation, child support, and all of the other signs of a respectable end to a marriage. Still, it is hard to explain to others that Diane has not met her father, nor will I introduce her to him.

"He and his family refused to acknowledge that Diane is his daughter. Instead, they claimed that I was having sex with others as well as with Jim. They obtained a lawyer to defend him against my claims. Their little boy was headed for a law career, and they wanted nothing like a young family to stand in his way.

"We moved away from my family after I finished the community college program, and we have a new life in this town. People just assume that I am divorced, and I don't correct their error. It's just simpler that way."

Many never-married women who become pregnant without forethought have an attitude similar to Ruth's. While movie stars such as Farrah Fawcett and Ryan O'Neal can have a "love child" or two, as have numerous other actors, including O'Neal's daughter Tatum, the less-prominent woman must make do with the old terms. You may have had an "accident" or you may have "slipped" or "goofed up," and you may be very sensitive to having anyone know that you were never married to your child's father.

You may not even be certain of the identity of the father.

"Sure, women in New York City, Chicago, or Los Angeles can make a statement by having a child when they want it," Ruth says with some amusement. "They can get lost in the city and their numbers keep them from feeling like two-headed giants. But don't expect it to be an easy act in a small town like mine. Even if you have a thick skin, and even if you have explained it well to your child, other adults and other children can make your child uncomfortable with their questions and attitudes. It is sad that I would probably have gotten more approval if I had had an abortion than I would if people knew that I'm a never-married mother. An abortion is quickly over and easily forgotten—by everyone but the mother. That's why other people can accept it so much more easily."

The terms "unwed" and "illegitimate" continue to infuriate Marion, who chose eighteen years ago to have her child without marrying.

"I suppose that some people viewed me as a fool. You know, 'getting caught' at the age of thirty-six and all of that. Those who knew me realized that I had made a conscious and deliberate decision to have a child—but I didn't want a husband in the bargain. They thought that I was crazy. For God's sake, I was thirty-six and the time for having a child was running out. One of my favorite authors, Laura Z. Hobson, the author of *Gentleman's Agreement*, had done so. Why couldn't I?

"Well, I could—and I did. I'll have to admit that having money and a secure job made life easier, but it couldn't ease the later pain of hearing my son referred to as 'illegitimate' and of hearing myself being called an 'unwed mother.' Referring to him as a 'love child' would have been no better, and it would have been blatantly untrue. He was no accident of passion. I chose his father carefully and never told him about Steven. Why should I? He is my child, not our child. Those words tarnished my happiness until I resolved to enjoy the decision that I'd made and to hell with the rest of the world!"

Maintaining the Image You Choose

Unless you have told your child that her father died while she was an infant, or that your marriage ended before she was born, you may have to come up with the answers to a few tricky questions once school starts. Your son or daughter may be perfectly comfortable with the truth that you have never been married, but other children will ask questions that your child may find uncomfortable. Be prepared for such questions, and prepare your child. Remember that the rest of the world is still more familiar with losing a father through death or divorce. Not having a father in the family from the outset is another story.

This won't be the first time that you will have to come up with answers that are no one else's business but your own. The chances are that, despite the claim of a tolerant society, you have already had to justify your decision to have your child without an accompanying husband. Parents, friends, coworkers, and other "interested" parties tend to be curious about your reasons for taking on what many view as a phenomenal job, that of raising a child alone. Their range of concerns may vary from fearing that you won't be able to handle the emotional and financial responsibilities alone to worrying that you will always have to live with the stigma of having had a baby "out of wedlock."

"My parents pleaded with me to have my son's father put his name on the birth certificate, and to have him acknowledge my son," recalls Sara, a thirty-six-year-old computer analyst. "I didn't need child support, and I didn't want a husband. All I had wanted was a child. I didn't tell my parents, but I chose to become pregnant with a married man because I knew that he would be hesitant to claim his child once he knew. I was right. I ended the relationship once I was sure that I was pregnant. When I ran into Jerry six months later, I was very pregnant and smiling. He looked frightened at first, but neither of us mentioned anything about my 'condition.' Very casual, you might say."

Many never-married mothers feel good about their decision, and they also feel good about themselves. Having confidence in yourself is important because others will only respect you to the extent that you respect and value yourself. Your decision to have a child without being married was made for any number of reasons. If it was a conscious and deliberate decision, then you already recognize that you are a strong and decisive person. Even before your child was born, you were faced with making the explanations to family, friends, and coworkers—or you made the decision to tell others that no explanations were needed.

Either way, your inner strength and your sense of self-esteem were already tested by the time your child was born. Why then should you find difficulty in answering others who ask about your child's father? You don't have to tell curiosity seekers anything when they ask. If too abrupt an answer makes you uncomfortable, keep in mind that your questioner is guilty of rudeness if he or she has tried to pry into your past without justification.

In a similar manner, your dating behavior and other actions do not have to be tailored to suit the people around you. Rather, your concern should lie with the welfare of your child and with your own well-being. Outsiders soon tire of prying when they find that their questions will get them nowhere.

Sex and the Never-Married Mother

"Some never-married mothers don't have difficulty reentering the dating scene because they have never left it," observes Dr. Marge Steinfeld. "Younger women may just resume their dating patterns soon after the birth of their children, so there isn't the same problem of reentry that the divorced or widowed mother may experience. Still, these mothers do feel more hesitant than divorced or widowed mothers in telling new men that they have a child. They become slightly embarrassed because they feel that they have to 'explain themselves.'"

Depending upon the man, you may find that you will be more uncomfortable in telling him that you chose to become pregnant rather than simply allowing him to believe that you were "caught." There are many men who may be hesitant about becoming involved with a strong woman who could choose to make so monumental a decision alone. Such men would prefer to believe that you were a victim of heated passion, a passive rather than an active participant in the choice to have a child.

You won't know in advance what the reactions of any man will be, but you can lessen the tensions and the potential for an uncomfortable rejection if you consider a man's own personality in advance. A weak, dependent man, whether macho on the surface or not, needs to feel in control. Your sense of control and feeling of confidence in your decision threatens that control, and he will most likely express disapproval. Men who have a strong sense of their own worth will be more likely to look at you as a woman, a single mother, however you achieved that position. In some cases, women have found that the men they date are actually pleased that they have never married.

"Tim congratulated me for my courage," says Rita. "More important to him was the fact that I didn't have the complaints about a messy marriage and divorce, or the many complaints about child support and visitation arrangements that he had heard from the divorced women he had dated. His one relationship with a widow had also left him with bad memories because he felt that she constantly compared him with her late husband. My never-married status was welcomed."

Unusual? Not as unusual as you might think. A man first meets you and gains an impression about you from the way in which you interact at the outset. By the time he learns that you have children, whether it is five minutes into the new relationship or five weeks, he has a picture of you in his mind. The way in which you view yourself goes a long way in determining how he views you.

If you are proud of your efforts as a mother, if you are comfortable with your decision to become a never-married mother, and if you value yourself highly, this will be communicated without words to the men that you meet. And you should be proud of yourself, comfortable with your decision, and value yourself highly. You should respect yourself because you have made a decision and you are standing by that decision.

To be honest, you also have to realize that not all men will have the same attitude as Tim, who actually welcomed Rita's never-married status. Some will think that you were reckless. Others may view you as being immoral (yes, even in 1987). Still others will be condescending in their attitudes.

Medieval as these attitudes may be, you have to face the reality that many men, however sexually active, still feel a sense of inadequacy about their ability to compete with a woman's former lovers. Others view women as being either "good" or "bad" girls. "Good" girls marry and produce children while married. "Bad" girls are sexually active outside of marriage and they "get into trouble." Other men, more relaxed in their attitudes, may accept you themselves, but they may have great hesitation about telling their family or friends about your never-married status.

None of these men are worth worrying about should they reject you because you are a never-married mother. You should not have to feel that you must justify yourself, punish yourself, or submit yourself to someone's condescending attitudes. There are enough attractive and intelligent men who will like you for yourself and who will see in you a woman of value, a woman whose capacity to love is great enough to have braved motherhood without the support of a husband.

But what do you do about dating, romance, and sexual relationships? To a great extent, once you have gotten beyond the problem of individual personalities, you will face the same difficulties as divorced and widowed mothers. Finding the time and the opportunity for romance will present the same problems, and you will have to exercise the same cautions regarding your sexual relationships. Most of all, you have the same right as all single mothers to enjoy satisfying romantic and sexual relationships and to find fulfillment in your life.

6

What Is the Age Gauge?

"I feel as if there is a yardstick that applies to single mothers as they grow older," says Carol, a thirty-eight-year-old divorced mother of two daughters. "The more over the age of thirty that you are, the less your chances of finding a man and having a successful relationship. Ask me. At thirty-eight, I'm an expert."

Many single mothers would agree with Carol that some type of process of elimination appears to operate to prevent single mothers in some age groups from meeting and mating with appropriate men. There is more to the age factor than merely the availability of men, however, and you should realize that the way in which you meet men, how you will carry out your relationship, and the factors that influence your decisions are very much based upon your age.

Younger single mothers have different needs than older single mothers, and they both have different qualities to offer the men that they meet. That's why the age gauge that seems to measure a woman's potential for success with men should not be viewed as a deterrent. Instead, it is a useful way of guiding you in focusing on your wants, needs, and potential for romantic success.

Age and the Availability of Men

"There just aren't enough eligible men to go around," moans Christie, forty-four years old, widowed and the mother of a teenage daughter. "I attended a singles' gathering a few weeks ago that was aimed at professionals in their thirties and forties. The ratio of women to men was awful, about eight to one. There are just no men available in my age bracket. They're all married, gay, or insane. Well, nearly."

The same grumbling appears in groups of women in their twenties. On the other hand, women in their fifties and sixties can be heard to grumble that men in their age range are all looking for women in their thirties and forties.

How can anyone ever meet her match? She can't if she isn't flexible in her requirements for a man, and she won't if she isn't willing to put age aside when considering her potential partners.

In general, there is a greater availability of men in their twenties and in the mid-forties and older than in their thirties and early forties. This is because many men are married by their late twenties, and they usually remain married, happily or otherwise, until the crisis of midlife throws everything, including their marriages, into turmoil. In addition, men in their sixties and older often become widowers, and they, too, are added to the available pool of men. As a result, there are certain specific age categories of men that are available to single mothers.

This doesn't mean, however, that if you are in your late twenties through early forties you should give up seeking a romantic relationship. Rather, you must realize that this staggering of ages does not present a true picture of the romantic possibilities available to you. What it does mean is that the single mother should be flexible in regard to the age of the man that she seeks.

The younger single mother often has an easier time attracting men and developing relationships than does the older single mother who is forty or more. The emphasis in our society upon pairing older men with younger women does give you the greatest advantage for finding romance if you are a single mother in your late twenties and early thirties. Even though men in your age range are not plentiful, you will find that men who are in their forties and even fifties may make good prospects for romance. In addition, the never-married men of your age and slightly older will more likely be attracted to you than to single women of their own age who have no children.

Does this last statement surprise you? It shouldn't. Men who have put off marriage as they have built their own careers may be ready to settle down when they reach their thirties. Although they may also be ready to start a family, they are also vaguely suspicious of a woman who has reached her thirties and only now wants to begin a family.

They may be concerned about the still-debated dangers of having a first child when a woman is over thirty-five years of age. They may also be fearful that a woman who has had a thriving career for fifteen years and who has not already experienced the responsibilities of motherhood may be an unhappy and resentful mother.

If you are a younger woman, you may also find that men in their late fifties and sixties will be suitable even if you are a young single mother with young children. Don't count out the divorced or widowed man with grown children. He may be not only eager to have a young family, but he may also want to produce more children as a means of rejuvenation for himself.

This doesn't mean that the younger single mother has an inside track on finding romance. For every man who welcomes a ready-made family, there are numerous others who will view your situation as being fraught with difficulty. If you are divorced and your children are young, then a man will foresee years of unpleasant negotiations and child support as a part of your joint future. With all of life's other hassles, why should he add more?

On the other hand, single mothers over forty may find that they may be more in demand than they think by men their age or older. Most often, their children are already teenagers, and there is a good chance that they will not want more children.

For divorced men who are burdened by child support payments and by their guilt for not being with their children, older single mothers provide a more suitable choice. A woman in her twenties or early thirties might still want to have children, and her present children will be younger and need more time and care. This makes her less desirable to many men. Those men who have dated single mothers over forty also point out that a woman with older children will most likely have established or reestablished herself in a career, so the financial aspect of dating an older single mother is also more attractive.

Of course, as with the younger single mother, there are many older single mothers who will be unsuccessful in their search for romance. Women in the older age brackets may have greater difficulty in attracting men of their own age because of society's emphasis upon youth. Many men want to date and to romance younger women because such relationships make them appear virile, however old they may be. Further, when a man of forty, fifty, or sixty dates women of his own age, he is reminded of his own age and of his own mortality. What does this mean for you if you are in your forties, fifties, and older?

It means that you have to stop looking at the men who are your age and older, and you have to start looking at men in general. You may find that a man five, ten, or twenty years younger than you will be attractive and attracted to you. As one man who was dating a woman fifteen years his senior said, "Older women know themselves, they have experience, and they have developed compassion. They also know what pleases them sexually and they communicate this to a man. That cuts down on the time wasted in fumbling."

When you are seeking romance, be flexible in your requirements. There really is no "appropriate" age range within which to look.

Age and the Sources of Romance

Although romance may be found with men of any age, many single mothers have found that where you find romance will differ according to your age.

"When you're twenty-eight or thirty, you can go almost anyplace to meet men and you'll fit in," says Tina, a fifty-two-year-old widow with one grown daughter. "But a singles bar at my age? No way! I did go to one once with my daughter, who is twenty-nine and just divorced, and I felt awful.

"I looked around me at all of those searching and strained expressions on the faces of young and not-so-young women, and I became depressed. There were a few men my age in there, very few, but they were all coming on to women in their thirties. Neither my daughter nor I stayed very long.

"I've also tried dating services and found that their selection of fine but older men is very poor. What I've realized is that you really have to depend upon chance meetings, the introductions of friends, and relationships in church or similar activities to meet men at my age."

"I don't even like the singles bars," confesses Tina's daughter, the divorced mother of a two-year-old son. "One place that

I do find helpful are the discos that have special age nights. One night they do the thirties crowd, another night it's for the forties, other nights they mix. That type of atmosphere is less of a meat market than the bars, but it still isn't aimed at the older single mother. I think that my mother's chances are better through personal introductions or chance meetings, as she suggested."

In addition to choosing different ways in which to meet men, older single mothers and younger single mothers differ as to their willingness to take a chance on love again. The hesitance of the older woman may be the result of one of several factors.

The older single mother is still more likely to be widowed than divorced. In many cases, widows have had happier marriages than divorced women, and they will take longer to try to find another man to replace their husband. In some cases, a widow's husband may have died after a long illness during which she nursed him and took on a range of other responsibilities. For these women, the prospect of marrying a man of their age or older whose health may soon require such care is frightening.

"I don't think that older women make romantic commitments less frequently than younger women because there aren't enough men to go around," states Gena, fifty-eight years old and the widowed mother of three grown sons. "More often, I believe that we choose not to make such commitments because of our own wishes and desires. I know that I'm not too eager to find a man my age or older and marry again because I feel as if I've just gotten my freedom. My marriage was good enough, but my time has never really been my own. It's time for me to take a look at life!"

What Gena says is true of many older single mothers who have discovered that divorce or widowhood in their late fifties and sixties does not plunge them into a panic to find another man. Instead, they find that they have been given a new opportunity to discover life and to take control of their own activities. These are freedoms that many older single women do not want to give up.

"I know that it is uncharitable," says Minnie, a sixty-six-year-old widow and mother of two married sons, "but I feel that I have more than paid my dues after nursing my husband through a long illness. At this age, most of the men that I know are beginning to complain about one ailment or another. All right, I know that I'm no chicken myself, but I have my health and I want to use what's left of my life to travel and relax. What if the man that I marry suddenly becomes an invalid? I'll be in the same prison all over again."

Age and Living Arrangements

"I can't get pregnant anymore, so what do I care if we live together or get married?" asks sixty-three-year-old Ann, a widow with two sons. "I don't want to lose my pension, and I don't want the legal inheritance hassles, but I do want Jason. So I've told him to move in with me. Of course, my sons, those respectably married angels of mine, are horrified at the prospect. They live in other towns, but they claim that my immoral arrangement is embarrassing to them and that I should behave in a 'proper' manner. Forget it. I want the companionship, and I want it on my terms. At this age, let people talk—if they even notice!"

Ann's solution to the matter of living arrangements is one that many older women have chosen.

A younger single mother feels the need to be concerned with the opinions of her former in-laws, the school, her neighbors, and her own parents when deciding whether to marry or to just live with a man. Although many will defy tradition, many more refrain from living with a man because of the repercussions that such arrangements may have for their children and because of a concern for future children.

Once a woman is past childbearing, the issue of unexpected pregnancy becomes a moot point. She can feel free to settle down and live with a man when children are not a factor.

Age and the Influence of Children

"When my sons were young, I was the decision maker," recalls sixty-eight-year-old widow Verna. "The older they became, the more they tried to make decisions and to tell me what to do. I used to date whomever I pleased and spent my time and money as I wished. Now, my two wonderful sons are trying to tell me which men I should like and which men will be 'trouble' for me. These two guys have their own families, but they make the time to try to play the 'man of the house,' but I like playing that role. I have to remind them both that I'm the only boss around here."

Verna's sons are trying to substitute for her late husband, and they are playing a role that thousands of sons being raised by mothers act out. In their desire to support their mother emotionally and physically, Verna's sons are placing controls on her.

The younger single mother may be influenced by her children, but the manner in which this occurs differs substantially when children are young. If you are a younger single mother, you will find that your children will make you feel guilty without even trying to do so. If your work keeps you away from them for long hours during the week, you may be unwilling to spend your weekend or evenings in search of romance.

When you do begin to date, your children may cling to you, making you feel guilty and casting a pall over your plans. Further, if your former husband takes the children for visitation, you may be concerned that he will ask them about your social life and that their answers will create new hassles over support and custody.

Once you do begin to spend time with a specific man, younger children will also join in the relationship to a greater extent than older or grown children who have created their own lives. Such interaction can be highly gratifying if everyone involved works to create a total relationship in which everyone plays a role. As you may have already learned, when such a relationship is not approached with caution, young children can effectively sabotage their mother's plans for romance.

Can you predict how your age will affect your potential for success in meeting and mating? Probably not. Nonetheless, your age does make a difference in the type of man as well as the type of relationship that you desire. In addition, although you may feel that meeting men is more difficult as you grow older, you will find that the older single mother is often more free than the younger single mother in determining the who, what, where, how, and why of her romantic relationships.

There are many ways in which you can use your age, whether you are a younger single mother with young children or an older single mother with grown children, to your best advantage. Don't be afraid of the "age gauge." Put it to work for you.

7

Are the Men Still the Same?

"After nineteen years of marriage, I thought that I knew all about men and their habits," says Jill, forty-two and the divorced mother of two daughters. "I had a really out-of-date view of the way that men and women should act when they went out socially. You see, I thought that husbands stopped holding doors open or letting a lady enter rooms first because husbands were bored with the whole routine of marriage.

"I was pretty surprised to find that the whole man-and-woman scene had changed drastically since I was last on the market! Rather than the strong, protective men that I used to date, I found myself playing nursemaid to a variety of men who cried on my shoulder and who went out of their way to show me how 'sensitive' they had become to women. Bull!"

Jill's voice rises in contempt with that final expletive. She finds many of today's men to be a disappointment when she compares them to men past.

"Maybe I'm just a malcontent," says Jill. "Yet I find that there has to be something available between the 'man of feeling' and the men who make it clear that they are doing me a favor by going out with a woman who has a child. Men have been dazzled by the statistics on the male-to-female ratio, and even the most modest of men becomes a 'prize' to be won."

Many newly single mothers agree with her, even the relatively young single mothers who left the dating scene only a decade or less ago. We may be eager to find and to please a man who interests us, but we are not too sure what it is that most men today want from a woman or from a relationship. To complicate matters even more, it appears that many of the men that are available are not too sure of what they want.

Who Are These Strangers?

One point upon which many single mothers agree is that men today are a lot different from those that they dated before marrying. The women's movement, the higher visibility of women in formerly all-male careers, changing male and female roles, higher divorce rates, and the greater independence of women have combined to produce changes in the ways that men relate to women professionally and personally.

Such changes have been noticed not only by women who are resuming dating after decades. Rather, both younger and older single mothers recognize the differences when they compare the men that they dated before marrying (as few as five years ago and as many as forty-six years ago) with those that they have dated since being widowed or divorced.

What types of men can you expect to meet as you resume your social life and try to make sense of the 1980s man? The choice is diverse, although the men can easily be classified as being those you want to meet and those that you don't want to meet. Based on their experiences, many single mothers have found, however, that most men will probably fall into one of the following categories: the "new feminist" man, the "macho man," the "liberated man," the "sad sack," "the walking wounded," the gay male friend, the straight male friend, and the truly "liberated" man.

None of these categories is any more or any less desirable than the others, except to the individual single mothers who have dated men with specific characteristics. Thus, while the "new feminist" man may not be the man for you, his type may be just what another single mother needs and wants in order to fulfill her life.

Before looking at the various types of men who will be a part of your social scene, or whom you may have already encountered, consider what it is that the 1980s man may want from you.

What Do Men Want?

"Sex," answers Dale, when asked what she found to remain the same between her new dating life and her old, premarriage dating. "Sex, that's it. The men haven't dropped that little requirement, but they have made it more complicated. And, might I add, much more pleasurable, since today's men seem more adventurous in their lovemaking.

"When I went out with a man before my marriage eighteen years ago, I could be sure that he would 'try something' at the end of the evening. Then I would pull back and refuse. He would relent until the next time, when I might or not 'give in.'

"It's a little different today. With some men, there probably won't be a next time if I don't agree to sex on the first date. To top it off, though, I get this same rush at the end of the date from men who may spend the evening trying to impress me with their views about women and equality and the need for more 'honesty' between men and women. Honesty, as he's trying to undo my blouse?!

"This act is rampant among men who, like me, are in their forties and who have recently been divorced. They have been kissed by the rhetoric of feminism and just enough has brushed off on them to give them some command of the jargon and the theory. It's in the practice that they're weak.

"That's why younger men make better dates. They grew up viewing women as being equals and with no sex hang-up, so the end of the evening isn't an expected 'pay-off' to the younger man but more of a mutually enjoyed pleasure. If the situation somehow forces me to refuse the sexual nightcap, I find that the younger man is usually more gracious and understanding. He is also more likely to call me again. The divorced man of my own age becomes miffed, and I never hear from him again. Good riddance!"

Many of you who were married two or more decades ago and who are now newly single have probably had experiences similar to those of Jill and Dale in meeting the new man and the not-so-new man of the 1980s.

Although many women applaud the newly liberated male, there are many more women who grew up believing that men are the dominant sex, like it or not, and that they should be protective of women. If you have been out of circulation for two decades or more, you may also be shaken by the fact that many men who are accustomed to women earning as much as or more than they may now expect a woman to pay her own way on a date.

"Before I married Ted in 1963, I dated extensively," confides Mary, a forty-six-year-old widow with one married daughter. "Sometimes I would get tickets for a concert or a show, and I'd ask a man to go with me. Well, I never bothered to wonder who would pay for dinner before or for the drinks and snacks later. It was just expected that he would take care of all that.

"Things are sure different today, however, and I'm not sure that I like it. I recently received free orchestra seats to a new musical, and I suggested that a man with whom I teach join me. He accepted eagerly and we decided to have dinner before. When the waiter brought the check, my date slowly moved it over to my side of the table and indicated clearly in that motion that he expected me to pay for dinner. I was flabbergasted, but I kept my cool and pulled out my credit card. I can't even tell you anything about the musical because I couldn't concentrate for the rest of the evening. After the show, I asked him to drive me straight home, and I refused when he suggested a nightcap at my home. I felt so used, so worthless for having had to pay for the evening."

Beyond these examples, there are many more ways in which men have changed in the last few decades. If you are a younger single mother, still in your twenties or thirties, the men that you now meet may be the same as the men that you have always known. You were raised in largely the same fashion as they, and the same social events that formed your sensibilities also formed theirs. Thus, you may find little change in men in the last five years, and there will be few surprises. If you are dating newly single men who are substantially older than yourself, you may find that these men may not have experienced the social changes because their married lives were spent in a social milieu different from your own. You may have to work on overcoming what can only be called a serious "generation gap" between you and your older lover.

In the same way, if you are an older single mother who has begun to date after two decades, you may feel that you are out of step socially unless you restrict your dating to men of your own age who have also just reentered the singles market.

Even then, your dates may bewilder you by being men of the 1950s and 1960s who have packaged themselves for the 1980s.

What does the 1980s man want?

"I'm not quite sure what it is that today's man wants of me," says forty-eight-year-old Bev, a widow with three grown children. "What I have found is that men are not the homogeneous group that I viewed them as being when I last dated thirty years ago. The men that I meet today offer a lot more variety in their thinking and in the ways that they interact with me. This makes the choices a lot more interesting. It also makes dating a lot more frustrating.

How Do Men View Your Family?

They may keep their thoughts to themselves, but you can be sure that most of the men you will meet have formed opinions about single mothers. Unless you have kept the existence of your children a secret or your date chooses to ignore their existence, you will find that your children will inevitably enter the conversation. Sooner than you may expect, you will be planning for a get-together that will appear in your mind to be only one step below the harmonious heaven of "The Brady Bunch."

Men, however, do not always view children in so favorable a light.

"I've never met the children of any woman that I've dated," says Brian, a handsome, twenty-six-year-old, bearded young entertainer. "That's not one of my priorities. I look at a woman. She looks at me. Something clicks. When I ask her out, I don't first ask if she's a single mother. If she is, then she knows enough to arrange for her children's care and that doesn't involve me. I go out with a woman for herself. Besides, the four single mothers that I've dated so far haven't made any move to involve me with their kids. They were looking for some fun. We danced, drank, and made love together. Strictly adult entertainment. The kids had no place in that."

Women who want to involve their children in their romantic relationships often find that they must find their way slowly in bringing all participants together amiably. Some men are hesitant about suggesting meeting your children or taking the kids to dinner because they may just not be comfortable with children. Other men may view the relationship as being only temporary, and they will not want to get too deeply involved in your family life for reasons of their own comfort. More sensitive men who consider the relationship temporary will not want to become deeply involved in your family so that your children will not be hurt when a breakup occurs.

Even in the less frequent cases when a man will whole-heartedly welcome your children on trips to places of interest or to dinner, you may encounter surprises. He may welcome them, but not the added expense of entertainment and food. Therefore, if you know in advance that a man is living on a limited budget because of child support payments or other obligations, you should be prepared to assume all of the costs for your children—or cancel the junket. This isn't the stuff of which romance is made, but it can surely save a lot of red faces and sullen silences if you settle this before you start out.

Although such arrangements work out well when you are only going out sporadically, they can become irritating if the relationship develops into either a living-together arrangement or a marriage. Men who insist on a separation of expenses during courtship usually want to keep it that way even after they have begun to share a household with you and your children. You may consider this to be fair, and you may agree to always pay for your children whenever your new family goes out to dinner, to the movies, or anywhere else. Before you write that promise in stone, think further into the future. Would you be comfortable with so structured a division of responsibility? Does this separation of "yours" and "mine" in regard to your children make you feel as if they are being excluded from the "ours" of the relationship?

Such questions may seem to be premature when you are dating, but that is the best time to sort out the answers. Women who decide to "let nature take its course" often find that they have courted disaster.

"He is handsome, intelligent, and comfortably well off," says Andrea, thirty-seven, of her man of seven months. "I know that I'm being unfair to him, but I also view him as being incredibly cheap. Oh, when we're out together dancing, having dinner, whatever, he spends lavishly. The best wine, good food, everything. But when we take my daughter out with us for a rare dinner, things change drastically. Greg pays for me and himself, and he expects me to pay for Jenny. I have tried to cancel some of our dates of this sort when the support money hasn't arrived and payday is too far away, but Greg always convinces me to go. Then I have to raid all my emergency sources for money. He tells me that he really likes Jenny but it is the principle that he stands on. Greg feels that Jenny's father should be supporting her, and so the money for her entertainment should come from him. I feel terrible for my little girl because she knows about the arrangement, even though I've tried to hide it. Greg's position makes her feel unworthy, but he is right, I guess. Jenny is her father's responsibility."

Greg is not all men. Many of today's men view a single mother's children as being undifferentiated from their mother. They come as a "package deal," and the man assumes responsibility for all expenses when the children are along. In cases in which a divorced man can barely afford his own expenses, the single mother offers to share the burden or they make different plans that will avoid the divided expenses.

Other men, like Greg, view a single mother's children as being necessary burdens that must be assumed if the mother is to be won. Don't consider this to be too harsh an assessment because you will run into your own share of Gregs as you date. Personal whim rather than financial necessity dictates the manner in which he treats the children. Having the single mother retain financial responsibility for her children maintains his sense of detachment, and it may also increase his role of power in the relationship. They remain her children, her responsibility.

What do today's men want? Who can really say? No two men are alike. No two single mothers are alike. And when any two partners begin a relationship, the possibilities are endless.

8

What Are Your Choices in Men?

Men are everywhere, and they are not always as different from the types of men that you used to date before you married. In some cases, their thinking remains the same as it was twenty years ago because they have also just reentered the social scene. In other cases, you will be dealing with cases of arrested development. In any event, don't count on any consistency in character among the men that you meet.

You will find that the men to whom you find yourself most attracted, and by whom you are found most attractive, will be those who suit your needs at the moment. Depending upon your personality and experiences, you may want to become romantically involved with a "new feminist" man, a "macho man," a "liberated" man, a "sad sack," a "walking wounded." Each of these types of men requires something different of a woman in a relationship, but they all do represent an opportunity for romantic pleasures. You may be personally turned off by several of these types, but there are other women who gravitate toward such men. As the saying goes, "Different strokes for different folks."

But what if you are not looking for a romantic or sexual relationship right now? Perhaps you want to enjoy the company of a man who will place no sexual demands on you but who provides a definite male presence in your life. What can you do? Are there any such men?

Yes, reply many single mothers emphatically. You may choose to have one or several "friends." Both straight males and gay males who genuinely like women can fill this role. Both the gay male friend and the straight male friend can be your buddy, your confidant, your shoulder-to-cry-on, and your intellectual adversary. Such a man will listen to your problems and share his with you. He will be your companion, your escort, your sounding board.

The difference between the two is that sexual tensions may always overshadow your relationship with a straight friend while sexual tensions usually never enter into your relationship with a gay male friend. To expect sexuality to be a part of either relationship is self-deceptive since they are essentially asexual relationships by their very nature.

Romance and sexual pleasure should not be your goals when you seek out "friends," but that doesn't mean that sex and romance will not rear their lovely heads. A straight male "friend" may very well turn into the lover that you've always wanted. If he doesn't, you will have lost nothing. Instead, you will have gained a better idea of the man who would make the ideal romantic partner, someone who can be a friend and a lover to you. He is the truly "liberated" man.

The "New Feminist" Man

Although often termed the "new wimp" by those who want to disparage him, the "new feminist" is a man that many single mothers find to be highly attractive and very desirable. He is a man whose consciousness has been raised, and as a result he works to treat women as his equals in all areas of life. Because he has become sensitized to the ways in which women have been made victims in society and in the workplace, he is very careful to have exorcised all sexist language and actions from his daily life.

"I don't like the term 'new wimp' at all," declares Meyra, a thirty-five-year-old divorced mother of two. "My husband used to view me as nothing more than a body, with little intelligence and no value outside of the home. It's wonderful to be with a man like Tom who will listen attentively to everything that I say, and who will go out of his way to keep from treating me or referring to me as anything less than his full equal.

"I find that his emphasis upon the cerebral rather than the physical aspects of what constitutes manhood has had a strong influence on my eight-year-old son, David. In the past, David would put up his fists and fight at school at the blink of an eyelash. Now, however hard it may seem, David has been trying to settle disagreements by talking. The other kids are not on the same plane, so it's going to take some time until he will be able to avoid the fighting altogether. But he's trying."

For women who have never been taken seriously by the men in their lives, the "new feminist" man is a welcome relief to know. Tender, compassionate, and nonsexist, he is a lively, intelligent companion.

"That's the right word, companion," asserts Darlene, a forty-two-year-old widowed mother of one son. "I can talk, joke, think, and debate with this man, but I find it hard to make love with him. Isn't that crazy? Here he is, tender, loving, and eager to grant me the orgasm that has been declared my right, and I find myself treating him like a brother. He has been through analysis, he reads feminist criticism, he has had his consciousness raised, and he is very sensitive to my needs.

"So why can't I reciprocate when he takes me into his arms and tenderly begins to caress me?

"Why not? Well, I think that he tries too hard outside of the bedroom to show me that he can be a nurturer and an equal. When we're in bed, I continue to look at him as a nurturer and an equal, somehow asexual."

Not all "new feminist" men are the same, nor are all of the single mothers that they date. Some women prefer the consideration, the tenderness, the sensitivity, and the compassion of this type of man both inside and outside of the bedroom.

"He's good for my kids, who have a decent role model, while I have a pleasant lover who also respects me," declares one woman.

Other women lose patience with the sometimes excessive sensitivity that the "new feminist" man shows regarding their roles as women. They are also turned off by the fact that treating women like equals must, of necessity, exclude the little niceties that many women miss but no longer expect, such as having doors held open, preceding a man into a restaurant, having a cigarette lit.

"To tell the truth, he finally got on my nerves," says one widowed mother of her "new feminist" boyfriend. "I am working and raising my children alone with no insurance money as a backup, so I know the hard facts of life in the workplace. At the end of a difficult day, although I love being pampered at times, I did not want someone emoting with me, sharing with me, or generally getting in my way when all I wanted to do was take a drink, soak in the tub, and talk with my children. There is a limit to my own sensitization to my plight and to my role as another female victim of society!"

The "Macho Man"

The "macho man" seemed to be a symbol of the 1970s, a time when singles bars abounded with hairy-chested men whose shirts were unbuttoned to their navels to expose the ever-present gold chains and medallions of every sort. Several companies must have made their fortunes by selling toupées for the chest to men whose chests were smooth and bare.

Clint Eastwood and other screen stars portrayed the "strong, silent man" whose actions were straight and sure, but whose words were minimal. Scoring was in and affection was out.

If you were single in the early 1970s, you most likely dated more than a few "macho men" whose collective goal was merely to add notches to their bedboards. The tone was cool, and "connecting" was the aim.

Does the type sound familiar?

Today's "macho man" is a distant cousin to his 1970s counterpart. The swagger is still the same, and so is the penchant for basing his masculinity upon physical prowess and upon his exploits. The exploits, however, have changed.

A greater openness about Vietnam has brought a new "macho man" out of the closet. This type has been heartily encouraged by the proliferation of Vietnam War movies.

"He could have been the man that I dated last before marrying Jim in 1974," remarks Kate, thirty-three, the widowed mother of Alex, eleven. "The look is surely different, and thank God for that. I never could stomach a bare, hairy chest and the clanking of the medallions and chains that went with the un-buttoned shirt. It is the attitude that hasn't changed. Today, however, that attitude seems to be based on some tie-in to heroic exploits and such.

"A man who exemplified this type was recently introduced to me at a friend's party for her daughter's graduation from high school. The man, a cousin of the hostess, tried to engage me in heavy conversation even as I backed away and tried to escape. In a rumbling voice, with minimal lip movement, he made the usual small talk, then, out of the blue, started with 'When I was in 'Nam.' I knew then that I could either stay and suffer through factual and fantasy heroic deeds, or I could beat a hasty retreat. I chose the latter."

Vietnam is not the only source of adventure for the new "macho men." Many engage in activities that are designed to test their physical abilities, and the "macho man" is always pushing his courage to the limit. For the single mother and her children, the "macho man" may provide a welcome sense of exaggerated masculinity—at first.

"I loved the feeling of being with this very masculine man who could make even facing a courtroom appear to be heroic," recalls forty-two-year-old Amy, divorced with a ten-year-old son. "My ex-husband is very low-key, and he tried very hard to give me the space in which to develop my own independence and talents. He is very sympathetic to the women's movement and has gone through the whole consciousness-raising process. Well, I found him boring.

"Merle, on the other hand, had a very strong sense of his masculinity, and he tried to dominate me from the outset. He is an attorney, and he advised me, protected me, ordered me, and dominated me. My son Tim loved having him around, and he soon began to imitate Merle's swagger and his aggressive attitude. It was all very novel, at first, and the 'macho' actions brought back pleasant sensations of being a child in a home dominated by my father.

"The romance of the 'macho man' soon wore off as I realized that I was expected to give up a lot to keep my man and to keep my man happy. Being dominated lost its attraction when I found that I was expected to curtail my career responsibilities and become the submissive woman."

The "Liberated" Man

Single mothers who have dated the "liberated" man describe him as a marriage between the "new feminist" man and the "macho man"—a feminist Archie Bunker. If the possibility staggers the imagination, read on. You may find that the "liberated man" has already crossed your path.

"My first reaction to Al was 'Is this man for real?' " laughs forty-six-year-old Marianne, the divorced mother of two sons. "I am an investments counselor at a large bank, and my responsibilities are rather extensive. Most of the men that I meet are married. The men who aren't married are either much younger than me or freshly divorced and still feeling the pain. When that rare single, apparently angst-free man of my own age comes along, I sit up and take notice.

"That's why I sat up and took notice when Al came along. His name is actually Alfred, and he may look like an Alfred, but he thinks and acts like an Al when it comes to women.

"He owns a small corporation that does business with our bank, and he is also an old friend of the vice president to whom I report. One day while waiting for my boss, he marked time by wandering around the offices. My door was open, and he spoke to me briefly. Later, in the elevator, he asked me to have dinner with him. That was my first encounter with the 'liberated man.'

"At first, I thought that he was trying to impress me by talking about the laws that protect women from discrimination and by his enthusiastic support for the equality of women. The more that he talked, however, the more that I realized that his brand of equality was more an offensive tool that he saw as being professionally useful in keeping his former wife and all female companions 'in line.'

"When we spoke about women and career, he expressed a strong feeling that all women should work and support themselves. When we talked about women and rights, he said that all women should have the rights and responsibilities of men. So far, so good, I thought. As I probed deeper, however, I learned that while I was thinking in terms of careers and personal relationships, he was thinking in terms of divorce settlements, women who 'pull their own weight' in a marriage no matter how many children they have, abolishing support laws, outlawing abortion, and a range of other horrors.

"As you have gathered, his stance on the liberation of women was based on the manipulation of feminist rhetoric with the aim of absolving himself and all men of the responsibility for the well-being of women. He viewed himself as 'liberated' because he had freed himself of the old male-female roles in which the male considered the protection and support of the female to be his duty. He was free of the old stereotypes, or so he thought."

You may not have yet met a man who could meet Al's level of callousness and total lack of humanity. Nonetheless, you have probably come into contact with others who exhibit the same anger against women to one degree or another. Such men mask their anger behind seemingly encouraging and supportive statements.

Do any of the following comments, made by coworkers or companions, seem familiar?

- "Hey, I wasn't going to insult her by offering to change the tire."
- "I don't want to patronize her by giving her special treatment."
- "Women are better money managers, so she really can make do without that raise."
- "I know that you're having a hard time financially, but you independent women land on your feet."

Have you noticed that most apparently complimentary statements made by "liberated men" usually leave a bad aftertaste? The "liberated" man places women in a double bind. He seems to support the idea that women should be independent and self-sufficient, at the same time that he gives out definite signals that they should somehow be punished for their independence and self-sufficiency.

Single mothers who have encountered the "liberated" man have found that this type is usually an older, formerly married man who has been unable to rid himself of feelings of anger about the end of his marriage. Not all men in their fifties and older have this attitude. Many men have welcomed the change in society that has encouraged women to take control of their lives. For men who have experienced real or perceived hurts as a result of broken relationships or marriages, such changes may be threatening. Some men adjust, while others, like the "liberated" man who is "all for women being liberated," turn mean.

No one can tell you that any one type of man is better than another, but the experiences of single mothers seem to indicate that the "liberated" man should be placed at the bottom of the list of choices for relationships. That is, unless you find constant putdowns to be amusing.

The "Sad Sack"

The "sad sack" is a male who believes that he has suffered severe battle damage at the hands of a woman or women. He turns to you for comfort, solace, salvation, and to find a listener to whom he can pour his heart out because "you're not like all of the rest." Whether he is divorced or never-married doesn't matter. What does matter is that the "sad sack" has a lot of tears to cry, and he's looking for a sponge to soak them up.

His litany of hurts can take hours for him to recite. If you've got the time, he's got the tears.

Does this attitude sound uncharitable? Shouldn't you reach out to this poor man and offer him someone with whom to share his troubles? Isn't it an act of mere human kindness to offer comfort to the suffering? Well, yes. But you may regret your charity after you realize that the "sad sack" is a professional at self-pity, and he is also quite adept at making everyone who has ever slighted him appear to be a villain.

"Frank was such a pitiful creature when I first met him," recalls Joan, thirty-eight years old and the never-married mother of a ten-year-old son. "Having never been divorced, I had gained all of my impressions about divorce secondhand. So at dinner the first night, when Frank immediately launched into a list of the injustices that his former wife had managed to perpetrate, I sympathized with him and consoled him. He was so distraught, and nothing that I tried to do seemed to comfort him. At the end of that first evening, he looked at me with his sad eyes and told me, as he held my hand, that he had not met such a warm and tender woman in a long while.

"I was flattered, and a fool because I agreed to keep seeing Frank over the next few weeks. As we made dates, and he failed to keep them and didn't call for days, I began to suspect that I was being emotionally used. When Frank felt in need of some sympathy, he would see me and cry his heart out. When Frank was feeling fine, I never saw him.

"I finally became annoyed with weepy dinners and long, miserable evenings with this poor, put-upon creature. After one particularly intense burst of emotion and a diatribe against women, from which I was naturally excluded, I finally told him that I was through playing sponge. No man or woman had the right to subject others to such prolonged misery.

"Frank's face reddened, and he told me that he had been deceived. He told me that I was no different from the others. As he stormed out of the restaurant, I thought with amusement that I had become one of the villains in his litany of hurts. Let someone else listen to his long, sad tale of misery."

The "sad sack" is pathetic, but he does require an intensive nurturing that may be very satisfying if your need to nurture is strong. The difficulty lies in his repertoire, which changes very little as the months roll on.

The "Walking Wounded"

The "walking wounded" is the personality opposite of the "sad sack." He really does suffer deep emotional scars from having lost at love and from having lost people that he has loved, but his means of coping is to hide it all inside.

The "walking wounded" will not pour out his heart to you. In fact, he may not even talk to you aside from the pleasantries of strangers. He has been hurt, and he doesn't want to be hurt again. As a defense against this, the "walking wounded" develops a protective shell around his heart and works hard to block out all attempts at affection.

What makes this man so attractive to single mothers? In part, it is the air of mystery that seems to surround his refusal to talk about his tragedies. He is also attractive because he appears to be impenetrable, and the challenge is exciting. In addition, in spite of his tough exterior and unemotional demeanor, the "walking wounded" appeals to the nurturing instinct of many single mothers. We like to view him as a hurt little boy who needs lots of love, our love, if he is to heal and to become whole again.

"Todd was a block of ice when we first met," says Megan, the divorced mother of a son and a daughter. "He was all business in our encounters, which were business nonetheless, and he never cracked a smile. I looked at him as a mystery in need of solving. No one in our firm, at least no one in my immediate circle, knew very much about his personal life except that he had been divorced some time ago and that he had a daughter listed as a dependent on his medical insurance file. Talk about snoops.

"When I was assigned to work with him and two other architects on the plans for a new city building, I resolved that I was going to penetrate that shell. I found him to be both physically and intellectually attractive. Maybe the mother in me also had something to do with it. He seemed to be trying so very hard to keep his distance from everyone, and I was determined to overcome that distance. But I had to move very slowly.

"The project required that the four of us put in long hours, and we worked on a tight schedule. As the only woman in the group, I felt a little hesitant about calling my children in the evening to just check in and to give them my love. My feelings were accurate because one of the married men did grumble the first time that I left to call my children. To my surprise, Todd spoke up in my defense. Later that evening as we left for home, I thanked him for what he had said and he merely shrugged. I decided then that the best way to get through the barriers around Todd would be to play up my role as a mother when we were alone.

"At the odd times when we worked at a desk apart from the other two, I would ever so casually mention something about one of my children. He just nodded without comment at first. Then one evening after about a week, he responded to a comment of mine by mentioning his daughter. I kept as cool as possible as I gently drew out more information about his daughter. Sooner than I thought, we actually began talking casually about something other than the city building.

"That was the start. I won't bore you with the details, but that night was the beginning of a new life for us both. We now see each other socially, and our children have become friends. It has been six months, but Todd is still protective of his feelings at times. You see, his wife had not only left him but, in rage, she had taken their daughter, who was only a toddler at the time, then abandoned her on the road. The betrayal and, yes, the anger against women had been bottled up inside him for a long while. It will take some time to eventually work it out. In the meantime, we have become genuine friends, and so have our children."

Under the shell of the "walking wounded" may lie a warm and loving man who needs to have his faith in humanity and, more specifically, in women restored. Such a man may be gruff-voiced and bearish in appearance, but he will run from you like a frightened child if you seem to threaten his carefully constructed defense system.

On the other hand, you should recognize that not all of the men who appear to be members of the "walking wounded" are men who have been emotionally hurt by a former wife or lover. In some cases, the man who appears to be intensely introverted and distant, or even hostile to women, is grappling with a long-standing distrust and dislike for women that may grow out of his childhood relationship with his mother. Such men often have deep-seated problems that require professional therapy. Your understanding and love alone will not suffice.

How do you differentiate between the two? If a man is openly hostile to women, if all women are openly downgraded, if he appears to have a grudge against women yet has never married, you can reasonably assume that this is one man who should seek help beyond what you can offer.

The Gay Male Friend

The gay male friend who likes women can be a sensitive and comforting man who will escort you, spend hours on the phone with you, and share your interests without asking for romance in return. He is very much like the pal who told you his most intimate secrets and with whom you shared your secrets without so much as a hint of sex to spoil the effect.

Usually well-educated, financially comfortable, and articulate, a gay friend can afford to squire you about town when you are feeling low or send you extravagant gifts when you don't want to face anyone but your children. Your children won't be threatened by your relationship because there are no sexual sparks flying, and no intense passion clouds your thinking. Although you can have all of the social benefits of dating with a gay male "friend," you are spared the often time-consuming aftereffects.

"I was too busy getting my career straightened and nurturing my children to have the time to become involved in a romantic relationship," recalls Doris, thirty-nine, the mother of a boy and a girl. "Although I wanted a social life—you know, dancing, laughter, sharing secrets—I didn't have the time to spare to really build a relationship. There was no spare time for angst over romantic misunderstandings, and I couldn't take the time to do all of the wonderfully romantic things that make romance exciting. Rebuilding my life and making life better for my children were my main goals—for the time.

"Luckily, James came along to offer me a pleasant and less energy-draining alternative. I am the news editor at a small newspaper, and he owns a small clothing store in town that caters to a very elegant male clientele. He made me laugh the first time that we met at an awards dinner, but I had no desire for him. I didn't know that he was gay, but he didn't turn me on when we met, and that puzzled me. He's good-looking, well-dressed, and moderately successful; and we really had a good time talking. By the time that the dinner ended, we had told each other quite a lot about ourselves, so he knew that I was not at all interested in finding a lover at that time. He told me later that we had gotten along so well and he had enjoyed himself so much that he decided to call. Well, he began to call, and soon I called him when I felt low. We had dinner about once a week to 'catch up,' and we really became great pals and at one dinner, James admitted he was gay. I said I had thought so and that it made no difference.

"We don't see each other now except for a brief greeting when we meet accidentally. James broke off our friendship rather abruptly when I became romantically involved with the man I am now dating. He may have sensed that we have a passionate sexual relationship, and any fool could see that I am madly in love."

Doris accepted her relationship with James as being just what it was—an asexual friendship in which both partners really cared about each other but in which neither had romantic designs upon the other. Some single mothers make the mistake of falling in love with their gay friends, even though they are fully aware of the man's commitment to his lifestyle. In the back of their minds is the fantasy that a man is gay because he hasn't met the "right" woman.

The single mother in love comes to believe that she is that "right" woman. Rather than to accept the friendship for what it is—a mutually supportive relationship that may very well be filled with true affection—the obsessed woman takes it upon herself to transform her gay friend into a heterosexual. In most cases, she loses her friend because she has violated their unspoken contract.

The Straight Male Friend

The straight male who is a "friend" can be both the most wonderful man that you will ever meet and the most frustrating. This friend may or may not excite passion in you, but he will be available to hold your hand through a crisis, to have dinner with you when your children visit their father, and to help you over the emotional rough spots. Like the gay male friend, he is what you may have called a "pal" when you were a child, and he very much resembles the kind of boy who was part of a group of high school friends who never dated but who did everything together.

In short, the straight male friend seems to be every woman's dream of a big brother/confidant with whom sex is permissible but not mandatory. This type of friend is a man who is seen more frequently today as women have entered many formerly all-male professions and as women have come to speak the same language as men. Of perhaps greater importance is the realization by most people that men and women can be friends, not only lovers.

The straight male friend is not necessarily a "new feminist," although he may display some of the same sensitivity. In fact, he may sometimes exhibit the behavior of the other types of men, depending upon the circumstances. What does make the straight male friend different from the other types of men that you meet is his interest in you and his concern for you as an individual.

"I doubt that my former husband was half as concerned with my happiness as Dennis is," observes May, forty-eight, widowed and the mother of a teenage daughter. "It isn't that Jim was cruel or anything like that. He was just indifferent to my feelings. As long as the meals were on the table, the clothes were ready, the house was clean, and I was sexually available, life was fine. His role was to provide, and mine was to use wisely what he provided. We lived contentedly for the twenty-three years of our marriage.

"Having a man for a friend is a welcome change. Dennis calls me to check on my 'emotional temperature,' to give me news, just to talk. When we go out, we are constantly talking, sharing ideas, and sparring verbally. I laugh a lot when I'm with Dennis, and my daughter has told me that she has never seen me looking and acting so alive."

"So what's my problem? I should really have no problem, but I do. I don't understand myself. Dennis is someone that I can call at any time and for any reason. If something must be done on my house, if my car won't start, if I'm lonely, whatever, Dennis will be here as soon as he can. We have fun when we go out. Everyone tells me that we're a great couple, very compatible. Well, one thing is missing. Sex.

"There. I've said it. I miss having a sexual relationship. Dennis is everything I want in a man, but he has no interest in adding sex to our relationship. No interest whatsoever! Whenever I have raised the issue, he reminds me that we have so much else and a sexual relationship might destroy the rest. He's afraid to chance it, and when I'm with him, I agree with him. However, when I'm alone, well, I think that he's wrong.

"I could discreetly see another man just for sex, but that would hurt Dennis and I would feel as if I were committing adultery."

Single mothers who date men who are "friends" frequently run into the same problem of risking the pleasures of friendship for the passion of sex. Most such relationships cannot continue as before once a sexual relationship begins.

That does not mean that sex will destroy the relationship. In some cases, the addition of a sexual dimension to a deeply committed friendship serves to heighten the feelings and commitment that a man and a woman have for each other. In a very special sense, sharing all aspects of their lives enriches both partners and provides an added dimension of security and contentment for the single mother's children.

On the other hand, you must also consider the possibility that a sexual relationship will destroy the earlier relationship that you have built. The reason for this does not lie solely with either partner, nor does it depend upon the quality of the sexual activity.

Psychologists observe that two people who have built a relationship upon the asexual qualities that underlie a friendship may find that sex makes different, additional demands upon them. These demands may overshadow the earlier and important reasons that fostered the friendship, and sex may take a central role. As a result, a new magic may appear that reflects the sexual passion and excitement. The old magic of friendship cannot compete with the intensity of this new magic, and many relationships change.

Dennis might be wiser about his friendship with May than she realizes. He, too, may want very much to enjoy her sexually, but he might fear losing the friendship that they have built up over so many months. In time, if the two continue in their friendship, a greater closeness will develop that should make the bond between them so strong that sexual love can also enter their relationship without any threat.

This doesn't mean that the men with whom you enjoy romantic and sexual relationships can't also be your friends. Quite the opposite. The blend is very precious, and it is one of the most satisfying of relationships that you will find. The man who can be both your sensitive and loving friend and your passionate and satisfying lover can only be the "truly liberated" man.

The "Truly Liberated" Man

The "truly liberated" man is a rare find. He honestly loves women and respects them without having to refer to one ideology or another to excuse his beliefs. Unlike the "liberated" man described earlier, he doesn't see the striving of women for equality as a reason for men to shift responsibility. Rather, he sees the achievements of women as being part of the natural order of human life, although not in such grandiose terms.

Women are not the enemy, nor are they inconsequential. For the "truly liberated" man, women are friends who can also be sexual partners.

Such a man stands out among the men who use a variety of acts to make their way in daily life. He is usually comfortable with his own feelings of being a man, and he doesn't have to prove his masculinity by acting "macho." He can be very tender when the time is appropriate, but he isn't overly sensitive to women's plight, like the "new feminist" man, nor does he depend upon the crutches of a difficult past or an impossible present, as might the "sad sack" or the "walking wounded."

In essence, the "truly liberated" man combines the qualities of a straight male friend with the romantic and sexual passion of a lover. He is an ideal who may well emerge from the friendship, often quite by accident. When it happens, finding the "truly liberated" man is a nice surprise indeed.

If you are just beginning a social life after several years out of the dating world, you will certainly find that men are different from how they were even a decade ago. They want more from women, and many of them expect to give more to the women that they date.

Women, too, have changed. You have changed since you were first married five, ten, twenty, or more years ago. You may not be meeting the same type of man as you met then, and that is all for the better.

9

Where Will You Meet Men?

"I kept wishing that I had been divorced," remembers Rhea, a former widow, now remarried, whose two sons were only five and seven when her first husband died. "To me, being a widow meant having a greater responsibility to my children because I was their only parent.

"Never mind that never-married mothers have to go it alone and the divorced mothers are often the only stable influence in their children's lives. In my fear of reentering the world of men and romance, I tried very hard to hide behind what I saw as my responsibilities. I agonized over making the first move out of my period of formal mourning. How could I do this to my in-laws? How could I do this to my husband's memory? How could I do this to my children?

"If you had asked me what it was that I thought that I was doing to all of these people, I would have no real answer. Still, the guilt was monstrous. I'm glad that I finally agreed to attend one party where I knew that the hostess had invited a man for me to meet. The matchmaking was a disaster, but the evening served as my reentry into life."

Planning Your "Debut"

You should start planning your "debut" even before you are comfortable with the thought of seeking romance again. Becoming "ready" for romance may require some complicated rethinking of your life and relationships, as we discussed earlier, and you need not necessarily be ready for love when you decide that you are nonetheless ready for life.

The sooner you begin thinking of going out again, the easier it will be for you to overcome the real and imagined obstacles that can block you from finding the happiness that you deserve. As many women have found in their own lives, postponing your social life indefinitely can lead to the development of patterns that will keep you locked into your unmarried world. You can't just sit back and tell yourself that fate will take its course. You have to make the effort and create your own fate.

Where will you begin?

You can start by becoming comfortable with taking an objective look at the facts of your life. Being a divorced mother is different from being a widowed mother, and both are different from being a never-married mother.

There are a few stereotypes to obliterate before we can really begin talking about making a "debut." As you read earlier, psychologists feel that the different circumstances surrounding the end of the marriage in divorce or widowhood make an important difference in the willingness of women to actively pursue a social life afterward. In addition, important differences exist between the woman who is a never-married mother by choice and the never-married mother who accidentally becomes pregnant but who nonetheless chooses to keep her child.

The divorced mother may have negative feelings about men and marriage, asserts psychologist Dr. Victor Solomon. Still, as psychotherapist Dr. Marge Steinfeld has observed, the divorced mother may want to connect sooner as a means of assuaging her anger and hurt, and to get back at her former husband.

The widowed mother, on the other hand, usually has very positive feelings toward marriage and toward men if her marriage was a happy one. At the least, she often feels that she must display positive feelings toward her late husband and the marriage, and she often comes to believe that the marriage was happy even if it wasn't. To do otherwise would be disrespectful to her late husband's memory, and it would not sit well with family and friends. Given these positive feelings, the widowed mother may be more genuinely open to men and romance than might the divorced mother, but she may also delay her "debut" longer out of the fear of showing disrespect for her husband's memory.

The never-married mother, because of differences that result when a woman deliberately chooses motherhood in contrast to the woman who accidentally becomes pregnant, has a totally different approach to the "debut." In many cases, no "debut"' is necessary because many never-married mothers have never stopped dating.

As Dr. Solomon has observed, "The single mother by choice could possibly have incorporated the idea of an ongoing relationship with a man or men into her plan of becoming pregnant. She may have wanted the pregnancy to lead to marriage. The 'caught' mother, on the other hand, usually continues with the mate selection process and will want to aim for marriage." Of course, both types of never-married mothers may have negative feelings toward men as a result of their experiences, however different, and they may both opt for lives without a man.

Then what of the "debut"? In general, each type of single mother experiences her "debut" in a different way because of the different opportunities that exist for each. In spite of the recognition by psychologists that divorce is a loss that also requires a period of mourning in which the divorced mother must confront her grief, most people see divorce as being a less difficult experience than becoming a widow.

You have probably noticed that neighbors are quick to rally around the widow after her husband dies, but few people bring casseroles or offer to help you through your grief after a divorce. More often, couples who were your friends during the marriage may suddenly feel forced to choose sides between you and your former husband. Even more gruesome is the extent to which your married female friends may deliberately avoid you because of the threat posed by your single status. They may be afraid that you will entice their husbands away.

The Divorced "Debutante"

As a divorced mother, you will probably have to make your own opportunities for a "debut."

Not every divorced mother is out on the town the night after the legal separation papers are signed. Some haven't been out for even the first time by the date that the divorce is made final.

"Sure, I know that everyone expects the divorcée to be out swinging as soon as she has broken her chains," says Terry, thirty-seven, the mother of six-year-old Jeremy. "Maybe some can do that. I couldn't because Jemmy was so young when his father walked out. I owed him my attention and my time, and I'm glad that I did refuse to go partying with my single friends. Jeremy is a secure and happy little boy. I'll have time enough when he's a little older."

Terry has been divorced for two years, and it is only recently that she has even thought about a social life. Only now she is a little puzzled as to where to begin. Her old friends have long given up on her, and she has not made any new friends. She has been thinking of attending a meeting of one of the single parent groups in her area as a start.

More common among divorced mothers is the move toward a social life soon after the legal separation papers are signed. Male coworkers, old boyfriends, or family friends may move quickly to capture your interest as soon as the ink is dry. You may find that some men will even claim to have loved you all the years of your marriage, and that they would now like the opportunity to show that love.

Take these relationships for what they are—your debut into dating. But don't take them too seriously because you are barely beginning to end one mistake, and you won't have the time or the strength to unravel another.

One common "debut" among younger divorced mothers is the visit to a singles night spot with well-meaning friends who have taken it upon themselves to get you back into circulation. Singles bars, discos, or private clubs are popular with women in their late twenties through thirties because they offer anonymity while you can try out your rusty social skills. For older divorced mothers, such places can be little uncomfortable if they approach them with the serious intention of meeting someone with whom to begin a relationship.

"Some of my divorced friends decided that I needed a night out to start off my single life and to get me out of my self-imposed exile," laughs Jessie, forty-eight, divorced, the mother of two adult sons. "We went to a well-known night spot that is famous in town for its loud music and serious singles of all ages.

"Thank God that I was with a group of friends that planned to stay together all evening. I have never seen such desperation.

The younger women seemed to attract hordes of men, from men in their twenties to men of my age and older that were trying to look younger.

"The women in their forties and older who were there were holding up the bar, clutching their glasses, and trying to look interesting and interested. My friends and I had our own table, so we whooped it up, and I would say that my 'debut' was a roaring success.

"Had I gone there alone or with the intention of meeting a man, you can be sure that I would have fallen flat. Singles places are really demeaning for a mature woman, and you can quote me!"

The Widowed "Debutante"

The widowed mother often makes her social "debut" in a different manner. More compassion is often shown to the widow for her loss than to the divorced mother who has also sustained a serious loss. Because of this, many widows find that they are invited to dinner by friends soon after the funeral and other efforts are also made to include these women in social events. Although the widow may be perceived as a threat by some wives, and she is viewed as an "available" female by some husbands, death and grief create an aura of respectability that divorce can never match.

Thus, you will probably find that your "debut" will most likely be at the home of a couple with whom you were friendly during your marriage. You will have to prepare yourself for a few bad moments during the first such dinner or party.

Although you may have been to the same home and spent time with the same people before your husband's death, this will be the first time that you will be in this home, with these people and at a party, without your spouse. Memories of former dinners and parties will be awakened, and you may be tempted to leave moments after you arrive. You may also be forced to be "good company" for an unattached male that your hosts will invite with all good intentions.

Of course, you may want to "debut" under other circumstances. Rather than begin your social life as the unattached female at a dinner party, you may find that a church group will provide your first social event. Some widows choose to forgo social contact with friends until after they have tried out their skills in a new group, such as a single parents' group or through a dating service. Still others seek casual coffee dates with men in bereavement counseling groups.

You must begin your social life anew at some point, and the point at which you begin is your "debut." Not only is this your "debut" into dating, but it may also serve as your reentry into life.

Looking for Love in All the Right Places

Where will you meet men, now that you have taken the first step toward resuming a social life? Many women will tell you that men are all around you, but finding those who are interested and interesting is still quite a trick.

There are a lot of ways, both planned and unplanned, in which single mothers can meet men. Friends, family, coworkers, children, and casual acquaintances are all potential sources of introductions.

Church groups, school organizations, night classes, school reunions, single parent organizations, social functions, business functions, community services, and other group activities are also rich sources of potential companionship.

Turn around in the supermarket, and you might bump into a divorced, widowed, or never-married man who may be eyeing the plums and you at the same time.

Everywhere that you go, and everyone that you meet, is a potential source of introductions to suitable men. To take advantage of all of these opportunities, however, you have to be aware that they exist, and you have to be open to introductions.

"My son was having some difficulty in school in the months after Jim passed away, and I went in for a conference with the principal," confides Marla, thirty-nine, mother to sixteen-year-old Fred. "The vice principal, a new staff member, handled the conference because Mr. Haley, the principal, was called away for an emergency meeting.

"During the conference, Mr. Sutton compassionately listened as Fred and I talked about Jim's illness and the strain that we had endured. The grieving was over, but we were still feeling that loss, and he seemed to understand exactly what we were going through. I later learned that his wife had died three years before after a lengthy bout with cancer.

"It was agreed that Fred would be placed in a structured program to help him to catch up in the two classes that he was failing, and Mr. Sutton also enrolled him in a private counseling program. I was invited to call in regularly to monitor Fred's progress, and Mr. Sutton graciously offered to call me with progress reports. His concern impressed me, and so did his crooked smile.

"The progress reports became frequent, and soon Mr. Sutton, now Rick, called me just to talk. We talked a lot about our spouses and about ourselves, as well as about Fred. By the end of the school year, Fred was academically and personally on track again, and Rick and I were in love. Who would have expected that to happen?"

Taking the Comfortable Approach

Meeting and mating can happen in many everyday situations. Single mothers suggest that you will be more successful in meeting men who are similar to you in background and tastes if you are introduced by family members or old friends. This is because people who have grown up with you and who have similar backgrounds and standards are also more likely to be friendly with others who have similar backgrounds and standards. No rule is inviolate, but this is a common experience of single mothers who have met men through friends or family.

No one, however, can guarantee that a relationship that results from such introductions will be successful any more than other ways to meet men can offer you any guarantees. Still, relationships that grow out of introductions by friends and family, or by meeting people through your social circle, church group, or other special interest activity, stand a better chance for survival than the chance encounter or the broad-based search that is offered by computer dating services or through personals ads.

Having an acquaintance in common or a common interest is an important starting point for a relationship. Yet it is only a starting point that can guarantee nothing if there is no basis for a relationship. But don't turn down the opportunity to date someone who is interesting for the short term. Even if you feel that your new relationship has little chance for survival, don't let that feeling interfere with your fun. Also keep in mind that this relationship may lead to your meeting someone else who may be more suitable than your present partner.

Formal Matchmaking

Single parents' groups, dating services, and personal ads are other ways in which single mothers have met suitable men. A word of caution is in order before we go any further.

The ways in which to meet and mate that we have discussed thus far all provide single mothers with ways to meet men who will probably share their interests and who will also have similar backgrounds and life experiences. In many ways, the introductions through family and friends, and the meetings with men through familiar group activities, are prescreened because of the manner in which they occur. Single mothers who have taken these routes feel more secure that the men that they meet are relatively safe, relatively sane, and usually (if not always) unmarried.

These assurances are not always true of introductions made through single parents' groups, dating services, or the personal ads, although the fewest problems seem to occur from meetings through single parents' groups.

Single Parents' Groups

Parents Without Partners Inc. is the best known of the single parents' groups, and there are thousands of chapters located in communities throughout the United States. The common ground of being a parent would appear to offer you a good start with the men that you meet here, but you can't always count on this.

If you view single parents' groups as a foolproof means of meeting a man who can best understand your situation as a single mother, you may be disappointed. You see, such groups contain single parents with a wide variety of living arrangements.

The men may be divorced or widowed, custodial or noncustodial parents. Further, the ages of their children may also differ widely. You will meet men whose children are infants as well as men whose children are older than you. These points are worth considering if you hope to meet someone whose situation is similar to your own.

Most single parents' groups hold regular meetings and sponsor various social nights to allow members to meet and to greet each other. The range and diversity of activities naturally depends upon the people who make up each chapter. A more sophisticated group might hold theater parties, while picnics and potluck parties at members' homes might be more the usual fare for other chapters.

Unless you are a joiner, caution single mothers who have gone the single parents' group route, you will be dissatisfied with this approach to meeting suitable men. The intent may be social on the surface, but many of the single parents' groups also function as support groups. As such, they may offer you more than you want—and they will require more than you may be willing to give.

"I didn't want to talk about the problems of being a divorced mother," declares Vivian, twenty-eight, the mother of a ten-year-old daughter. "My whole purpose was to meet men who were also single parents and to start going out again. I thought that my daughter would be better off if I dated men who also had children. So I tried the local single parents' group. My mistake. The people there weren't exactly losers, but they had the loser mentality.

"The first meeting was a little corny, with the introductions and a little pep talk about single parenting. Then we were invited to mix informally. That's when I headed for the door. There were many more women than men, and the men didn't look too lively."

Vivian's complaint about the lack of men and the tone of the single parents' group is echoed by other single mothers, both widowed and divorced, of all ages. Although such groups may still have a strong following in some cities, many single mothers seem to prefer other ways in which to make contact with eligible and available men.

Such complaints are brushed aside by other single mothers who have found Parents Without Partners Inc. and similar groups to fill a need in their lives.

"At least I know that I don't have to pretend when I'm at a Parents Without Partners meeting or social event," says Lois, thirty-three, the mother of two sons. "The 'moment of truth' when you reveal that you have children is eliminated by the fact that everyone in PWP has children. I am not a woman who enjoys fast and anonymous sex, so the bar and regular singles scene is not for me. I like to meet men in casual, homey types of situations. In this way, I often find that the men I meet have something in common with me, and we can work up from friendship to anything else that we want. There's no pressure to continue if we find that we are not compatible.

"Parents Without Partners and other groups of their type are not without problems. Anyone can tell you that. I have spent more than one evening at a PWP party, cornered by a man who refuses to let me leave his sight. Sometimes the other members get on my nerves when they complain about minor problems with their children. But these are minor annoyances that don't compete with the security that I feel when I meet someone through PWP. It's not sexy and exciting, but it is dependable. I'm a woman who likes *dependable.*"

The Dating Services

Dating services are another means of meeting suitable men, but you have to be on your guard. This approach is frequently used by single mothers who are too busy in their careers or other activities to take the time to meet suitable men. Many busy women find that they can't find the men that they want. They contact dating services in the hope that a man who meets their requirements is also looking for love. Still other women are afraid of personal rejection, and they hope to narrow both their options and their chances of rejection by finding men who will meet their specific requirements.

Romances have blossomed between single mothers and men who have met through dating services. It is a more efficient, if impersonal, approach that separates the lookers from the seekers. Before you meet a man, according to the philosophy of the dating services, you will know that he is looking for a single mother with your qualities and characteristics. You should also expect that he will have the qualities and characteristics that you want in a man.

With today's more sophisticated videotaping procedures, lengthy questionnaires, required references, and high fees, it would seem that this system would be safe, secure, and effective. Don't count on that.

Not all single mothers who have gone this route would recommend using a dating service when you're looking for love.

"Their brochure promised that they screened all applicants and that what you read in the description of a choice would be what you got," relates Tanya, a forty-two-year-old divorced mother of four. "I wanted to stay away from a single daddies lineup, so I went with a dating service that catered to all kinds of singles. The questionnaire was impressive, and I answered every question truthfully. I even gave the names and ages of my children under the 'comments' section.

"When the service told me that there were five men who met my qualifications and who had expressed an interest in me, I was overjoyed. Four children are a handful, and I thought that these were five brave men.

"You should have been there. Number one was the opposite of my ideal physical description and he was fourteen years older than me. I had requested about a five-year difference. Number two hated children, and he snarled almost as soon as I mentioned mine. Number three was a fun date, and I almost fell for him by the third date. Fortunately, I found out in time that he was a married man who had lied on the application. The promised security check had, apparently, not been done. I decided not to meet number four, who sounded rather wheezy on the phone. I had requested 'athletic' and 'excellent health.' Number five began pawing me almost as soon as I entered his car, and I spent the evening pushing his hands away while he provided graphic accounts of his sexual conquests.

"So much for dating services. I am now happily dating a man whom my mother introduced me to, and my kids love him."

Your experiences with dating services might be better. They certainly couldn't be much worse than Tanya's experience.

Should you choose to try this means of introduction, use caution and good sense in selecting the service. Before you sign anything or give out any personal information to a dating service, make certain that you understand the way in which they disseminate information to and about applicants. You will want to remain anonymous to all interested parties until you are ready to meet someone.

Ask how carefully applicants are screened and request specific information as to how the applications are checked, if at all. If a dating service refuses to answer questions that relate to your security and safety, forget it. You are better off losing a chance at meeting someone rather than to run the risk of being caught in a scam.

Scam? Yes. Not all dating services are run by reputable people. Some exist for the sole purpose of gaining detailed personal information about single women. What they do with that information can range from the merely annoying to the overtly dangerous. Your caution should be increased by your concern for the safety of your children.

Personal Ads

Personal ads are less expensive than dating services, but they, too, offer you the chance to specify your requirements for a man and to advertise your own qualifications. Many single mothers who place personal ads are hesitant to mention that they have children for fear that they will lose valuable opportunities with men who usually ignore all ads mentioning children. Their hope is that such men will find, after they are acquainted, that they like their children. This dishonest ploy is common, and because both men and women cheat in their ads, it undermines the potential value of such self-advertising.

What do you say when you place an ad? You might begin by telling the truth, so that you will only attract the attention of men who would fit your requirements and situation. Your honesty may gain you less attention than might a more vague and evasive ad, but the replies that you receive will be more on target. How you construct the ad will tell your reader a lot about how you order your priorities.

Will you mention first that you are "vivacious, tall, and elegant," or are your status and number of children top priority? Do your children and family play a central role in your life, or are they mere addenda to be tacked on at the end? Are you looking for a playmate for yourself or a man who is compatible with your total family situation? Should he have children, or is it of no concern?

Begin your ad with words that convey the primary impression that you seek to project, then follow up with other information. Never, however, include your name, address, or telephone number—even if the publication permits them, and most do not. You must treat a personal ad as you would any other risky venture and exercise caution.

"I've had a lot of success with the personal ads in the local newspaper," states Jenny, a thirty-seven-year-old divorced mother of two daughters. "My first ads were lighthearted and funny, and I didn't mention my children in them. Because of my little omission, I usually had an uncomfortable time for the first few dates until I could finally tell the men about my daughters. In a few cases, telling them ended our dating, but others had no feeling either way as long as I kept the relationship free of children while we were together.

"When I finally did mention the children in an ad, my replies were way down in number but they increased substantially in quality. The man whom I am now dating was one who responded, and his reply caught my eye because he wrote about his children in the letter. I'd recommmend the ads if you're shy, as I was, and if you have a good imagination."

Love and romance are all around you, and so are interesting and interested men. If you want romance to enter your life, you must be open to men and be willing to begin living and loving once more. Even more important, you have to begin the process of meeting and mating yourself.

Eager friends will do their best to introduce you to one man or another, but you will soon find that their choices are more suitable for your friends than they are for you. On your own, you can languish as you wait for the next prince on a white horse to come along, or you can go out and find him.

If you decide to begin the hunt, you will have plenty of company among other single mothers. You will also have plenty of help, in the form of groups, dating services, personal ads, introductions. Some will be beneficial, while others will merely waste your time. If, however, you have already determined the type of man that you want and the type of relationship that will be best for both you and your children, you will have greatly increased your chances for success.

10

Are All of the Good Ones Married?

"Men should come with labels on them," laughs Bette, a forty-three-year-old divorced mother of two teenage daughters. "You know, 'divorced,' 'widowed,' 'never-married,' and 'married.' Especially that last one—married. It would save a lot of time and aggravation for me, at least.

"You eventually find out more than you need to know about a man, but you can waste a lot of time while you wait for the revelation that a man is married. Look, I was married, and now I'm divorced because my former husband used to omit that little bit of information when he met attractive single women.

"I don't want to have any part in making some wife miserable, so I try to find out at the start if a guy is married. Knowing about the others can also make a difference in whether or not I pursue a relationship. A little bit of truth in packaging wouldn't hurt."

Men. Are all of the good ones really married, as many single mothers might begin to suspect after a round of miserable dates with a collection of whiners, boozers, or womanizers? Can a single mother be compatible with any type of man, or must the divorced mother meet and mate with a divorced man, the widowed with the widowed, the never-married with the never-married, and everybody or nobody with the married man?

Are there rules for determining which man will be most suitable for you? Yes, say many single mothers, but you may find yourself making them up as you go along.

You may find as you date that you will always avoid certain types of men. The man that many single mothers love to avoid is usually the recently separated or newly divorced male. His angry and often hostile view of women in general and of his wife in particular makes any relationship aside from quick sex impossible. Even those divorced men who adopt more passive attitudes and who become either "sad sacks" or "walking wounded" fail to hold interest for long.

As one single mother said, "I had just about gotten hold of myself and I was sailing a fairly even course. Then, bam. I started to date Doug and his depression and ranting made me feel horrible again. He wasn't doing too well, and he dragged me right down into the dumps with him."

Other women have a similar reaction to having a relationship with a married man. They often become romantically involved with the man while they are at their most vulnerable after the divorce or the death of the spouse. By the time a woman realizes the complications that may emerge, she may be too in love to care.

Does that leave only the widowed man, the younger man, or the never-married man as potential candidates for romance? Well, no. You see, some single mothers find that a widower will frequently hold on to the memories he shared with his late wife, and getting even a toehold in his life can be a monumental task. Others find the possibility of dating a widower to be disturbing, especially if the man is young and his wife died young. Such a situation too strongly reminds a single mother of her own vulnerability.

Never-married men? "Yes," say some single mothers, while others refuse to date never-married men on the grounds that they are often too fussy, too set in their ways, not used to children. Such prejudice against this choice is not universal among single mothers. Many find the never-married man to be most attractive because he has no wife, either living or dead, and no children to compete with the single mother and her family.

Even the younger man comes under fire by single mothers as a potential romantic partner. Although most would agree readily that the sexual vigor of a younger man and his firm body certainly score him points as a lover, they also agree that people still do talk. Many single mothers who prefer younger men try to keep their relationship hidden and mainly enjoy their partner behind closed doors.

Are you discouraged by this brief examination of the men in the single mother's life? Don't be. There is no surefire guide for anyone to choosing the type of man who will fulfill you sexually and make a suitable romantic partner. It is all chance. You may find that a divorced man is perfect for you, whatever your own status. Other women may find that a relationship with a married man that promises only brief stolen moments of happiness is all that they want and all that they need.

What do you need? Consider the men who are available to you for romance, but remember that passion and romance are rarely rational and never reasonable.

The Divorced Man

When it comes to a romantic relationship with a divorced man, I have some good news and some bad news. First, the bad news. Divorced men can be a problem for all types of single mothers because, like the divorced woman, they may have negative feelings about both marriage and women. At the same time, the bruises received in divorce have left them groping for a way to rebuild their egos. Quick and anonymous sex is often the solution.

"Slam, bam, and no-thanks-to-you, ma'am, is the way that most newly divorced men want their relationships," says Lila angrily. Divorced and the mother of two preschool children, she had hoped to remarry soon after her marriage ended and the ideal choice appeared to be a divorced father. "I soon learned that divorced men just want one thing—straight sex. Now, I don't have anything against sex, but I do like to talk a little, get to know a person, and relax beforehand. Racing for the finish line just isn't pleasurable, but most of the divorced men that I've dated seem to be running the Indy 500. I always have the feeling that they want to hurry up and hustle me into bed early so that they can work on someone else for later that same night."

Single mothers, in general, have few encouraging words about divorced men. Because of their experiences, divorced men usually bear a grudge against divorced women. Their own wives may have gotten the house, a car, and alimony of $2,000 per month as well as child support while you have been struggling along on peanuts. This doesn't matter to the newly divorced man because he often perceives all divorced women as having fleeced their former husbands.

You may, indeed, have a lot in common with the divorced man, and you, too, may have had an unfortunate experience in regard to the financial settlement. This doesn't always penetrate the subconscious. Many divorced men tend to lump all divorced women into one category: bitch.

He may say that you're different from his former wife and you may be struggling along on little or no support. Still, there will be the inevitable comparisons. She took the children from him. (You have your children.) She took the house from him. (You may have gotten the house in the settlement.) She is eating him up alive with her financial requests. (You mentioned that you haven't received a support check in months.)

The widowed or never-married mother may fare slightly better because she has not had the experience of divorce. The divorced man will often be highly complimentary of the widowed mother's influence over her children and of her ability to "carry on." At the same time, he will ignore a similar determination and competence in the divorced mother. Yet the approach to sex appears to be the same with widows as with divorced mothers.

Now that you've had the bad news from single mothers who have dated divorced men, it's time for the good news. Divorced men aren't hopeless possibilities for romance, but they will require more understanding than might other men who have not gone through the trials of divorce.

First of all, not every man is in shock from his divorce, nor do all divorced men take their anger and hurt out on the women that they date. Some do. Learn to spot them early in the evening, and avoid them whenever possible. Having been hurt by another woman does not give a man the right to make your life miserable. There are more important sources of pain with which you must contend in your life.

In many ways, the divorced mother may find that a divorced man who is not carrying a grudge against all women is a good choice. Because his marriage failed, he is less likely to be judgmental regarding the failure of your marriage. It is highly likely that he has children, and this may allow your children to play a greater role in the relationship than if you were dating a man who has little or no experience with children.

Further, because his financial resources may be limited due to support obligations, he is less likely to want to do the town often. Because most of your socializing will be casual or even in your home, you will be more accessible to your children, and a more comfortable and natural relationship can develop.

Is there hope for a relationship with a divorced man? Yes, say single mothers, but you have to look long and hard before starting up with these men. Single mothers who have dated divorced men suggest that you don't date any divorced man who tells you that his marriage has just broken up. If he interests you, keep him in mind, but give him time to get over the initial pain and hurt. That may be cruel, but you don't deserve to become a surrogate ex-wife while he goes through the process of healing. And your children should not be subjected to the tense and irritable you that will result from a relationship with a man who is antagonistic.

The Widowed Man

Single mothers who have dated both divorced men and widowers enthusiastically recommend the latter. They claim that men who have lost their wives to death are usually more inclined to be looking for romance as well as sex and that they want less to score than to honestly get to know a woman. Although many more advantages to the widower exist, there is some bad news.

Widowers are usually, but not always, older than the average divorced man, thus their tastes in music, restaurants, and other entertainment may differ significantly from those of younger single mothers. Further, because they usually hold little or no bitterness toward their late wives, as might the divorced man who must pay support and who has been displaced from his home, they keep the wife alive in their homes and hearts longer. You may have to compete with the ghost of a woman who, as the result of death, has become the ideal woman with whom few could compare. Photos of the wife and mementos of the marriage will be placed throughout his home, and you will find that memories will crop up in your conversations.

Try as he may to avoid doing so, a widower will compare you with his late wife. Some of the comparisons will simply be to point out how similar you might be in your tastes, actions, or reactions to those of his late wife. Listen for the tone of the widower's voice to determine if the comparison is done in loving memory, as it well might be, or if he is recalling unpleasant episodes from the marriage. Are you being complimented or criticized? Knowing the difference can be important to your decision to continue a relationship or to end it quickly.

Nonetheless, there are generally more positive than negative aspects to dating a widower.

"Widowers are a different breed of male than the divorced man," observes Terry, a thirty-nine-year-old divorced mother of three children. "There is no bitterness, no 'digging' about divorcées, no dredging up old hurts. Better yet, because there is no ex-wife, a widowed father usually has his children living with him so he doesn't have any guilt or anger about my children. Divorced men have told me many times that they can't get close to my three because of guilt feelings about their own children whom they only see periodically."

This enthusiasm for the widower is shared by many single mothers who add that the sexual behavior of the widower contrasts sharply with that of the divorced man.

"A widower has to heal in a different way than a divorced man," notes Grace, herself a widow and the mother of two sons. "He isn't duty-bound to prove his virility and worthiness to the world by bedding every female in sight. Even though the memories of his loss may be painful, once he can begin talking about his late wife, it will probably be in tones of respect and sadness. You'll hear none of that anger and degradation with which a divorced man usually describes his former wife."

A very important difference between the widower and the divorced man is that the widower is not usually negative in his feelings toward women. He may have nursed his wife through a long illness, and this may make him wary of women who are frail or of older women who might become ill, but this does not mean that he will be negative toward you. Instead, because he may be raising his own children alone, he will more likely admire you for your efforts with your children. Rather than to probe and criticize you regarding child support, he will be aware of the cost in money, emotional stamina, and time that children extract. A widowed father could well become your greatest fan.

You can make this more likely if you resolve to like his late wife. She may be physically absent, but her spiritual presence can be strong, and this will influence the feelings of the widowed man. Single mothers who have dated widowers suggest that you encourage a man to talk about his late wife and about their marriage.

"He was thinking about her most of the time and sometimes the words would slip out," remembers Tina, formerly divorced and now married to a widower. "Whenever he slipped and called me by her name, he would become red and change the subject. I was embarrassed for him, then I realized that I needed to know about his late wife and the marriage if I was to get anywhere with him. So I began to draw him out and ask him questions.

"At first, Gil was very hesitant to talk, then he loosened up and a torrent of memories came pouring out. He was really very relieved to finally tell someone how he felt. Since that time, he hasn't called me by her name, nor has he spent as much time reminiscing. It is out of his system, and I am into his system."

The Never-Married Man

A man doesn't need to have been married, nor need he be a father to be a suitable partner in romance for the single mother. Still, single mothers report that there can be serious problems if a man has had no contact with children and if he has no understanding of the patience that both parties need in a marriage and in a committed relationship.

"He told me that I was handling my son all wrong," says Merrill, the divorced mother of a twelve-year-old. "Then he philosophized a little about how cooperation between parents results in well-adjusted children. It was all textbook stuff, but I was living real life! I was amazed that a man who had never been married and who had been in the world of adults for so long could act as if he had such expertise in these areas."

Many single mothers who have dated never-married men complain that they are made to feel as if they are going about this mothering thing all wrong. In part, the criticism that they receive stems from the belief by the never-married man that he can control his environment. Children appear to be only an extension of that environment. Any parent would question that assumption.

Furthermore, because they have never been married, such men may find it hard to understand why the widow might retain an attachment to her late husband or why the divorced mother still experiences pain as a result of the failed marriage. In the single world that is often the milieu of the never-married man, relationships that end are not mourned substantially and the ties that exist often do not bind.

If you are a widow, the never-married man may feel intimidated by your late husband, and he may fear ever being able to compete with the memory. If you were divorced and the process was messy, he may fear that you will project your anger onto him. Your children may scare him if they are older and protective of you, and they may annoy him if they are younger and need considerable amounts of your attention.

More difficult to accept is the possibility that the never-married man may consider himself to be somehow "too good" to be marrying a woman with children, even as he condescends to date you. If he is a professional in his thirties or older with substantial money saved, he may feel that he deserves a woman who has also never married and who is free of the emotional baggage of past marriages and of the burdens of children.

When you find a man who holds this attitude, don't even bother trying to prove him wrong. Forget him. He probably has reinforcement for his views in the person of parents, siblings, or friends. The time that you may waste can be spent in happier hunting.

If he is past thirty-five and never married, a man may be living a life of established patterns that will be difficult to change. Moreover, he may not be willing to change these patterns, and he may ask instead that you and your children make changes in your lives to suit him. That last point can end a relationship before it begins. While children are flexible, you and your children should not be asked to completely change your lives. Instead, the never-married man must be willing to meet you at least halfway.

Is the never-married man just an "old bachelor," even in his late twenties, and set in his ways? And if he is, does this make him an impossible choice for the single mother? Not necessarily. The never-married man can be flexible, given the right circumstances. You must open up communication if you really want a relationship to develop.

"Never-married men can really be the best choice of all," suggests Darla, thirty-five, the divorced mother of a son and a daughter. "They don't have ex-wives to upset them, and there are no children to support. In addition, they are free to be with my children without feeling guilty that they are cheating their own kids.

"I'm especially lucky that my son is ten years old and athletic. Most of the never-married men that I've dated keep their bodies in shape because they are 'on the market,' so they love to shoot baskets or pitch baseballs. Those who think that they're doing me a favor by dating a single mother often find that I strike first by refusing to make a second date with them. I make it clear that I have my own doubts about a man who is forty and never married, and that deflates their egos for a while."

Darla's attitude toward never-married men with overblown egos brings up several interesting concerns about the older never-married men. In a nation in which the average age at first marriage for men is 25.9 years of age, a man who hasn't married by the age of forty or more is usually scrutinized closely. Your mother may tell you that he's a "good catch" because he has spent nearly twenty years stockpiling his salary as a professional, but he bears closer examination.

- He may be gay but he has reached a plateau in his life and now wants children and a family, while discreetly continuing his other lifestyle.
- He may be emotionally immature and have the need to remain forever young by staying with old patterns and living arrangements made early in his adult life.
- He may hate or fear women as the result of trauma experienced in childhood.

On the other hand, a man who has reached forty without marrying but who now seems interested in a commitment may just have never met the right woman. He may have been cautious in his relationships and decided that his marriage would stand a better chance if entered into with a woman who met his requirements.

He may have been busy building an empire and now finds the time to look around.

He may have been happy with the singles scene but the 'big 4-0' birthday has made him feel that life could be better.

Never-married men? They are a good choice for the single mother who may find that her new love will welcome warmly his new, ready-made family. The best part is that he has no former wife with whom to compare you and no children against which to measure yours. He may be set in his ways, depending upon his age. He may also be overly stern at first, until he learns that children are fairly reasonable creatures. Be patient as your lover moves from living on his own to living with a family. Having to share his surroundings with children who are not always quiet on command, having to wait for the bathroom, just having to conduct himself as part of a family will take some time to get used to. Once he learns his way, your children and you will be very pleased with the results.

The Younger Man

A fifty-five-year-old man can walk arm in arm with a thirty-year-old woman without anyone giving them a glance, except in envy of the man. They can announce to the world that they are in love, and they can marry without anyone saying much more than "congratulations." The same can't be said when a fifty-five-year-old woman has a romance with a thirty-year-old man.

Why wouldn't any woman in her fifties want to have a relationship with a man in his thirties? The benefits to such a relationship seem fairly similar to those of the fifty-five-year-old man with his thirty-year-old girlfriend: sexual attraction. Women of all ages appreciate a firm male body, and the younger man can offer the additional lure of sexual vigor.

Why turn all of that down?

If you listen to what others will say once you do begin dating a younger man, you will hear a slew of reasons, most of them invalid. You may find that this disapproval is intensified by your role as a single mother because you, of all people, are expected to behave "with decorum." And decorum has decreed that younger men are off limits. Those who disapprove seem determined to take all of the pleasure out of life.

"I don't care what my mother, my friends, or my children say," states Susan, a fifty-two-year-old widow with two grown children. "Jack is exciting, interesting, and wonderful to be with. He is also fourteen years younger than I, and I love it! It's no one's business but ours, but a lot of people seem to be making our romance their business. We have been together for three years, yet I am still warned that he will leave me for a younger woman. The predictions are dire, but I have always loved adventure, so I'll chance it. With three years of happiness so far, a lot more than some people have in a lifetime, why should I worry about the future?

"I am lucky to have the present. I could be dating men of my age or older, and most of them would be financially better off than Jack. But they wouldn't be better in bed. Let's face it, a man in his thirties just has more sexual prowess available than a man in his fifties. His body is bronze and firm, and he is so free in trying out every way to please me. Men of my age never did that—and I can't imagine them doing so now.

"I feel as if I just began to live when Jack became my lover. It's good to feel so sexually alive after the years of struggle and of being the 'good widow.' No one is going to stop me from enjoying my reward."

Not every single mother who dates a younger man is as strong in the face of criticism. Still, a good many single mothers do date younger men, and for many of the same reasons as Susan. The differences in age can range from only three or four years to couples who are twenty or more years apart.

The younger man may be divorced, widowed, or never-married. He may or he may not have children. Rather than blaming age for the problems that they may have with their younger lovers, most single mothers feel that these other situations are often to blame for difficulties in their relationships.

"Difficulties? What difficulties?" asks Fran, forty-seven and the divorced mother of two daughters. "If a man is divorced, then younger or older he is going to have difficulties relating to me. If he's widowed or never-married, there may also be problems. But these problems will be the result of his past marriage and the existence of children—not because I am ten or twenty years older.

"My personal experience is that younger men, whatever their previous marital experience, are generally more compatible with me, and I am generally happier. The reason is probably the fact that I am honest with younger men. I don't look forward to marriage. I don't want any more children. I don't ask for permanence. All I want is a virile and passionate lover who wants to please me sexually. The younger men that I've known have been happy to comply.

"I'm presently having a relationship with a man in his twenties who is just starting his career as a bank executive. I've even fantasized about helping him, since I've been a bank officer for nearly twenty years. Oh, younger men, I love them."

Single mothers who date younger men point out that the sexual satisfaction and physical attractiveness of the younger man was what attracted them at first. Younger men are also more free in bed and willing to experiment. This is natural since many of these men grew to maturity in the 1960s and the 1970s, when sex had become a freely discussed and freely indulged-in activity.

To emphasize only its sexual aspects would trivialize the relationship. Although younger men are physically more fit and sexually more active than older men, these are not their sole sources of attraction.

"Tim never makes any snide comments about my career or my struggle to balance being a mother and a career woman," says Kathy, a thirty-nine-year-old divorced mother of two who is having a romance with twenty-three-year-old Tim. "He grew up with a mother who worked, and he has a really free outlook on life. He often gets home before me and begins cooking dinner and amusing my children so that they will calm down after their own hectic school day. When I get home, I am not subjected to the complaints or grumbling about missing shirts or other domestic disasters that I used to hear from my former husband. Tim knows the business world, and he respects my right to be in it. He's also a 'hunk'!"

There are many advantages to having a sexual and romantic relationship with a younger man. However, there is also some bad news.

The bad news about the younger man/older woman relationship is that too many people in the single mother's life may disapprove of such a coupling, and they will be more than willing to make their feelings known. She may be accused of wanting another son and of being a "mother figure." Others may say that she is "robbing the cradle." Her children may find that a man who is significantly younger might be close enough to their own ages to be upsetting to themselves and to their mother.

"I have to admit that I worried when Bill and I started dating," admits Fran. "He was twenty-six and I was forty-five. Not only was I so much older than he, but my daughters were twenty-four and twenty-two. They were dating men of his age. Naturally, I worried that they might label me a 'silly old fool' and think that I was in competition with them. I wasn't.

"Even more so, I worried at first that Bill would meet my daughters and find them more attractive than me. I agonized that he'd fall madly in love with one of them and leave me. It didn't happen. Bill is a very mature man, and he looked at my daughters as being my children. We have been together for two years, two glorious years during which Bill has repeatedly asked me to marry him. My fears were groundless. By the way, I do intend to marry Bill in a year or so, after my youngest daughter has married. It would be only fitting for me to wait."

Single mothers who date younger men sometimes do so because of the sheer lack of men in age categories that are closer to their own. This lack is made worse by the tendency of men to seek out women who are years younger, thus leaving the more mature woman without potential partners of her age and older. The younger man is a welcome choice and opportunity.

Relationships between younger men and older women are often of more concern to outsiders than to the two people involved. If the single mother and her romantic partner have a relationship that is built on a variety of shared interests, then youth and age don't even enter the discussion. But even in such cases, women have said that they feel uncomfortable when a song from their teenage years comes on the radio and they realize that their younger lovers weren't even born while they were dancing to it.

Younger men have younger friends, and this is also a source of concern to their older partners. For many women, social gatherings with the friends of a younger lover can be very painful, as the age difference then becomes very apparent.

"I could do anything, say anything, and be anything with Ken," says Jaimie, a forty-five-year-old widow with one son. "The criticism from my family and friends just rolled off my back, and I never thought about the sixteen years between us. However, when we went to a party of some of his friends last Christmas, I felt old and out of it. There were a lot of twenty-nine-year-olds like Ken. Others were in their thirties and some were in their early twenties! Here I was, the mother of a twenty-two-year-old man, trying to keep up with these kids. It was like looking into the mirror after a crying jag and seeing a crone staring out at you. Even though Ken said everything possible to reassure me afterward, I decided to end the relationship. Too bad. I really enjoyed being with him."

There are disadvantges to younger men, but there are also significant advantages, aside from the sexual. For one, life expectancies for women are still greater than they are for men, so it would seem logical for older women and younger men to couple. Further, single mothers today who are divorced, widowed, or never-married have to compete in a new world that requires them to be independent and self-sufficient.

For women in their forties, fifties, or sixties, this new attitude toward life makes them less likely to be satisfied with the roles that men of their own age usually want them to fill. A better choice is the younger man who has grown up in a society in which many mothers work and achieve. He is usually more understanding about a single mother's drive for success in her career and her need to support herself and her children.

Beyond these advantages is the simple pleasure that both you and your children may derive from being with a younger man who has not lived long enough to be jaded and bored with life and who still has the capacity and the energy to enjoy it to its fullest.

The Married Man

Because of his obligations and vows, the married man would not appear to be a viable romantic choice for the single mother. Nonetheless, many single mothers not only have romantic relationships with married men, but they actively seek them out.

"I'm not ready for a full-time relationship," says Maggie, a twenty-eight-year-old widow of two years. "My children are young, and I don't want to become involved with someone who is going to want a lot of my time. For now, a 'same-time-next-week' arrangement is enough to keep me aware that I am a woman, but it doesn't lessen my accessibility to my children."

Limited commitment, the desire to possess what already belongs to someone else, the lack of other choices—all are reasons for single mothers to date married men. Most women who have romances with married men are not looking for a long-term arrangement, and none of the single mothers who admit to such affairs said that they are hoping for marriage.

"First of all," asks Maggie, "why would I hope for marriage when I deliberately chose a married man? Even if I thought that he would leave his wife and family, I would never feel right about the marriage. If he left one wife and family, what's to stop him from doing it again?"

In contrast to such stopgap arrangements that make a romance with a married man a means of marking time until a suitable man comes along, there are single mothers who fall intensely in love with a married lover. For such women, affairs of five or more years are not unusual.

"I did not want it to happen," claims Serena. "Certainly, I had no intention of hurting his wife or his children, or my children. I just needed to have him, even if for only a few hours a week. After a few months, he started showing up at my home early in the morning, then after work at night. Some evenings, he told his wife that he had to work late, and he would have dinner here with my family. My daughters, now in their late teens, loved him. We went out with my sister and her husband and had a wonderful time.

"Everyone in my family knew that he was married, but he spent so much time with us that we thought that his wife truly didn't care. I couldn't imagine that any woman would be so blind that she didn't realize that he was spending long hours away from the house. How long could a man claim that he was working so many hours?

"It had to end, but I wish that it could have ended on a better note. Rather than violins and moonlight, the ending came when someone who knew about our affair called his wife and told her. When she refused to believe it, the person called her sister and laid out the whole story. Mark proved the kind of man that he was when he was caught in the middle. He denied that he could have anything to do with me and called me many obscene names on the phone. He swore to his wife that he had been blackmailed into the five-year affair. The worst of it is that she believed him. I may be better off without him, but it was fun while it lasted."

Romance with a married man isn't something that just happens. Instead, single mothers who have been involved in such relationships say that they were seeking such relationships. The limited time of the married man, his other responsibilities, and his inability to demand marriage are all reasons that some single mothers prefer married lovers to others who might be willing and able to plan for a future.

This attitude may be fine for the single mother, but it cheats her children who may come to look upon the married lover as a father. Their hopes may be falsely raised, then dashed when the married man must eventually return to his marriage and his acknowledged family.

If only a handy guide could be developed that would match you with the man who would best fulfill your needs as a single mother and as a woman. Not only does one not exist, but single mothers have found that their own views often change from relationship to relationship. A bad experience with one divorced man can temporarily turn a single mother away from all divorced men. On the other hand, chancing another relationship of this sort and succeeding will restore her faith in divorced men.

The best that you can do is to know what kind of relationship is right for you and to consider each man on an individual basis, whether he is divorced, widowed, never-married, or younger. The good men aren't all married—and the married ones aren't all good.

11

Is It Still Called Dating?

"I tried on a dozen outfits and none of them seemed right for the big night," remembers Jana, thirty-seven years old, the widowed mother of a teenage daughter. "Clothes were all over the room, jewelry was spilling out of the jewelry boxes, and I was frantic. My daughter stood calmly near the closet and commented on all of my choices. It wasn't until later that I realized that we were playing out a very uncomfortable scene of reversed roles. She was the mature mother, and I was the schoolgirl getting ready to go on her first date. In retrospect, that whole scenario is very scary."

Whether you have been out of circulation for two years or twenty years, the process of reentry is bound to be a little uncomfortable. Instead of being part of a couple, as you were while you were married, you now reenter the social world as a single. The small talk will be different, and so are the men. More important, you are also a mother, and you will have to deal with all of the images that others have regarding motherhood.

New Rules for Old

You may be five years older or forty-five years older than you were when you last went out socially with someone other than your husband. The rules have definitely changed.

Single mothers in their forties often find that they grew up with rules of behavior that seem primitive in the light of today's moral code. In the 1950s, many teenagers talked about sex, although in whispers, but a fairly rigid code of behavior ruled.

Kissing on the first date was officially out, but unofficially indulged in. "Necking" was only enjoyed after several dates with one boy. "Petting" was reserved for that "special" boyfriend, and often only after the two had officially declared themselves to be "going steady." "Going all the way" was a teenage girl's ultimate way to "prove" her love. The "good" girls carefully preserved their right to say "no," while "fast" girls who had sex with more than just their "steadies" were talked about by both their lovers and the "good" girls.

We can be grateful for the sexual revolution of the 1960s and the changing mores of the 1970s that made relations between the sexes more relaxed. For the woman who married before the "revolution" and who has only recently become single again, these changes can take some getting used to.

Even for the younger single mother, the old rules of courtship can be substantially different now that she has been married and has a child.

"He told me that I was sexy and desirable and that he couldn't wait to make love to me," recalls Laurie, forty-five, the mother of two teenagers. "Now, I am the last woman to turn down a compliment, but this man had just met me, and I do like to know someone's last name before going to bed with him."

She is talking about a man that she met recently when her friends decided to introduce her to today's social scene. To avoid throwing Laurie to the wolves by taking her to a singles bar or to another anonymous meat market, they chose to go to a singles party that was organized by a local singles organization.

"It really couldn't have been as bad as I remember," laughs Laurie. "The fault was really mine because I was expecting a slower approach and maybe a little courtship. This man set me straight right away. He told me that I should know the score, at my age and having been married already. A few minutes later, I saw him working on another woman on the other side of the room. I 'know the score,' all right. How can anyone with teenagers not know how sex is viewed today? Still, I have my own thoughts about sex, and I'm going to stick to them!"

Such experiences are merely accepted as a sign of the times by single mothers like Laurie who shrug and continue to choose their own paths. You have to have a strong sense of respect for yourself to successfully challenge the way that many men today tend to view the single mother.

Many single mothers find that some men feel that single mothers over forty should be grateful when a man buys them a drink or offers to take them to dinner. To some men, the single mother of any age is nothing more than a predator, eager to find another "meal ticket" and someone to raise her children. This brand of man is not the majority, but he makes the strongest impression on women who meet him because of his particularly offensive nature.

Because they take such negative views to heart, single mothers who haven't developed a healthy sense of self-worth may view themselves as being somehow "inferior" to other women. They are not as young. They are not as financially well off. They are not as free. Therefore, they may conclude that they are not as good.

Such thinking is self-defeating and should not be permitted to rule the way in which you interact with the men that you meet. Sex may be freely enjoyed today. The labeling of "good" girls and "bad" girls is only a memory. And you may be very ready, willing, and able to enjoy a full and satisfying sexual relationship with one man or with many men. The choice to have a sexual relationship should not be made because a man makes you feel grateful to be asked; nor should you look at sex as your way of keeping a man's interest. Whether or not you decide to enjoy the more sexually open spirit of the 1980s, the choice should be yours, made freely and without pressure from anyone. This freedom of choice may well be the best of the new rules.

Even though you may know them, making the new rules work can be another story.

Who Are You Today?

"When they called the whole man-woman thing the battle of the sexes, they were definitely right," states Myra, a forty-eight-year-old divorced mother of teenagers. "I feel like a seasoned soldier in the war, and I've just begun to date again. The problem is that the men who are available now don't know what they want, so I'm not sure of the image to project when I try to meet men.

"I met a wonderful man last week at a friend's party. Intellectual, cultured, debonair. Naturally, when we went to dinner a few nights later, I tried to portray the same image, and I did pretty well at it. I did so well that he told me that he hadn't realized I was so similar to the women with whom he works and whom I sensed he despises.

"He had watched me at the party before introducing himself, and he had gained the impression that I was fun-loving, lively, and sexy. On our date, he began relating to what he now thought was the real me, the act that I had created to impress him. What he wanted was the candid me and not the woman that I became for one night in order to impress him. I was too embarrassed to explain my little act, so I just said a quick goodnight and beat a hasty retreat!"

How should you act? Try to follow the old rule that never fails—no matter what your age.

Be yourself. Never try to second-guess a man's tastes and needs to the extent that you change your whole way of living just to attract him. Whatever your age, you just don't have the time, nor should you expend the effort that is required to fully meet every presumed requirement of another person.

Moreover, your attempts to perform a personality transplant can have disastrous effects on your children and on your home life. Role playing can be fun for the short term, but a woman who must bounce back and forth between who she really is and the role that will attract someone else will wear herself out and confuse everyone.

"My kids still tease me about being 'Mama the hot tamale,'" says Katy with a wry laugh. She feels fortunate that her children are old enough to have survived her temporary change of personality and that they can now joke about it. "When my husband left four years ago, I was totally crushed. My son was twelve and my daughter was fourteen, and I was thirty-five years old. I felt as if my life was over. Finito!

"A year later, I was a totally new woman—on the outside. My favorite magazine had carried an article about beating the divorcée blues, and one of the suggestions was to do a complete makeover of your appearance. Now don't laugh, but I really thought that looking different would do the trick. Then he would see, or so I thought.

"My goal was to go from hausfrau to hot stuff in five easy lessons. My hair was lightened and permed, nails were painted scarlet, and I started to wear sexier and more revealing clothes. As a result, I began to attract attention—from my children, my family, and coworkers. Have you ever seen an EDP supervisor with Fu Manchu nails? Well, neither had my superior, and those went quickly. The rest, however, stayed long enough to get me into hot water.

"With the new image came the conviction that I should be out in the world, looking for 'action,' as several of the other divorced women in my office urged me to do. I finally agreed to join them one Friday night, and we converged on a lively dance spot that seemed to be loaded with men. My new look attracted attention, and I soon had a few men around me. Me. The housewife and EDP supervisor having men milling around. I was impressed with myself.

"When I narrowed down the possibilities to one interesting-looking man, I settled in for some conversation. Forget it. He kept eyeing the neckline of the dress and raking his eyes over my breasts and thighs. After an hour, my 'admirer' asked me to leave with him. He told me that a 'hot tamale' like me must be dynamite in bed—and that's where he planned to head with me!

"I remember hearing him shout that I was a 'tease' and other uncomplimentary comments as I stalked out of the place. Since then, I have kept a lot truer to type and 'Mama the hot tamale' has been retired permanently."

The desire to attract a man may overrule a single mother's good sense when she considers the image that she must project. Men may have specific images of the divorced single mother, the widowed single mother, or the never-married mother, as well as the single mother who has one child as opposed to the woman who has five children. You can't control their perceptions or their biases, but you can control the way in which you allow these perceptions to affect your life and that of your children.

Five different men will have different perceptions of the single mother. It is not your job to act out their perceptions or to change your personality to suit their desires. If you are not a siren, don't act out the role just to meet men. Such role playing can be fun for a few hours or for a few evenings, but you may have to make such behavior a way of life if you intend to remain with the man that you attract with this role.

Can you sustain the act, if it is contrary to the more realistic you?

You must also give serious thought to how the "new you" will affect your children who have lived with the old you for some time. Changing your image does not always have negative consequences. You might find that your family life will improve as the result of changes that you make in your lifestyle and in your image.

"Cooking to me was a career, someone else's, a specialty that was not one of the experiences that I could list in my résumé," comments Vernell, a forty-two-year-old divorced lawyer with three children. "When I married, I made it clear that I was a professional whose specialties never could and never would include housekeeping or other domestic duties. My family had always had housekeepers for that. They were the specialists.

"After the divorce, life changed very little in our home because the house was run as it had always been run by the housekeeper, and I continued with my law practice. The difference was that my children did not have a father living in the house. Not that they had seen much of him. He was very busy and traveled often on business. Sunday was the day that he'd be out by the pool and fooling around with them in the water.

"Wouldn't you know that the man who would capture my attention after the divorce would be the complete emotional opposite of my former husband? He was from a big family that, although very wealthy, ate meals together, shared table talk, played sports, and generally behaved like a clan. He was shocked to learn that I rarely saw my children, and even more shocked to know that they ate their meals with the housekeeping staff because I was often too busy to join them.

"His mother had had a house full of servants, and she was busy with a variety of foundations and charities, but she still made a point of cooking at least one meal per week herself. She also made a point of assembling the family for at least one meal a day, even if that meal had to be a very early breakfast.

"That was strong competition, and I was determined to let him see that I, too, could exhibit some family closeness. After several lavish nights out, I suggested that he join my children and me for dinner one night. I would cook. Bad judgment call

on my part. I will never again view the cookbook as a surefire
guide to producing edible food. I ruined dinner and my ambition
made me an object of some amusement to both Phillip and my
children for some time.

"But I've had my revenge. A few weeks later, I told them
that I'd made some soup for our late-night dinner after a rigorous
workout on the slopes, and we had a marvelous evening of
togetherness. I intend to do it again sometime, but I have to
be careful about hiding the institutional-size soup cans that I
used!"

The point of Vernell's experience is not that she has come
to appreciate the importance of homemade food, for she hasn't.
Rather, for perhaps the first time in their lives, her children are
eating with family rather than with the servants. Phillip is important enough to Vernell that she wants to make changes in
her life, and it is her children who are gaining the greatest
benefit from that change. The introduction of a new man whom
the single mother wants to please may be responsible for bringing
about a welcome change for the entire family.

How Do You Date?

Dating as a single mother presents many more complications
than the dating you did before you were married. In those early
days, there were no baby-sitters to secure, no children to reassure,
and no last-minute emergencies to handle. Instead, your biggest
worries were that your pantyhose were run-free, your makeup
was well applied, and your outfit was appropriate.

You are not a teenager today, and you know it. So do your
children, and they will never fail to remind you to act your age
whenever you may slip.

"Oh, God, Mom," groaned the daughter of one single
mother when the woman emerged from her bedroom with the
"big shirt" and stirrup pants that are faddish among teens and
younger women. "You look awful in that getup, like you're
trying to look younger than you are."

Her mother actually was trying to look younger than she
was and apparently failing miserably.

Not only do single mothers sometimes confuse their outlook
on life with age-appropriate dressing, they also find that hastily
made dates often lead to confusion in the family.

"But you promised to take Cathy and me skating on Saturday night," wailed eight-year-old Jody to her mother, Dee, who had just announced that she had a date for Saturday night. "I hate that man, and I'm going to tell him so when I meet him!"

Caught in a crossfire of her own making, Dee called her date and pleaded for a raincheck, which she didn't receive. She spent Saturday night watching Cathy and Jody pick themselves up off the rink floor as they mugged it up for her. That incident convinced her that an appointment book was needed if she was ever to begin having an active social life.

How do most single mothers date? Badly, according to all accounts. To successfully coordinate family, job, and personal responsibilities with a social life takes planning and managing your time. Such planning, however, is something that few women seem to get to until they have had a few social disasters. The following suggestions from single mothers may help you in your planning.

1. A first step in organizing your social life is to make a firm rule that you will not say yes to anything until you are sure that the needed time is free. It is better to have to say "I'll have to check that, and I'll let you know in a few minutes" than to make two commitments and have to break one. In addition to disappointing one of your commitments, you will also aggravate yourself needlessly while deciding which commitment to choose.

2. Ask your children to check in with you before they tell their friends that you will be available for an activity. You have a life of your own, too, and it is not selfish to ask that your children of every age show consideration. Such consideration can go a long way toward increasing the time that you will have to enjoy life with your children and with your dates because the pressures of command performances will be removed. Allot time that you can really spare for dating, socializing, and sharing with your children.

3. If your children are young enough to require baby-sitters, compile in advance a list of people who are available on short notice, as well as those who need early warning. Do not call the same sitters each time that you go out, but make an effort to have all of the sitters on

your list sit for you several times. In this way, you are covered should an unexpected opportunity come up, and your children will not feel abandoned, because they will already know their sitters.

4. Make certain that the sitters have the telephone numbers of where you will be during various times of the evening, even of his place, should you plan on ending the evening there. The safety of your children should be a strong enough concern that you will not let petty morality prevent you from covering all points. If you feel uncomfortable in giving these numbers, then provide the sitter with the name of a relative or other responsible person who can adequately take your place should an emergency arise.

5. Take the time to make it clear to your date if you expect to return home that night, and let him know the time beyond which you cannot stay out. Does that sound like a curfew? It is a curfew, and one which you must meet more carefully than those that your parents imposed when you were in high school. If your children are young, then you know the value of a good baby-sitter. Getting home two hours after you promised that you would can upset a baby-sitter and make her less eager to sit when you may need her the most. If your children are older teens, then you may be worrying them if you fail to appear at the stroke of three, as you promised. Think of how you react when your children miss a curfew, and act accordingly.

Your child-care arrangements may be only a peripheral concern to the main event—the date—but it is an important peripheral that can sabotage your social life if handled poorly.

12

How Are Sons and Daughters Affected?

Dating requires that you make some important decisions regarding how and when your children will meet the man or men in your life, as well as how you will relate to them now that you have emotional interests outside of the home. If you choose to avoid the issue indefinitely by meeting your dates at their homes or at restaurants or the theater, you will eliminate the often uncomfortable moments spent in introducing your children and your dates to each other.

Don't consider this a long-term solution, for it isn't. You will eventually have to deal openly with your dating. Your children will realize that you are dating even if you make up excuses for your evening absences, and they will want to meet the people with whom you are spending your evenings. Your children will also be affected, either positively or negatively, by the mere fact that you are dating.

Before discussing how to make these introductions less painful for everyone, you should consider the different ways in which your children of different ages, male or female, are likely to react to your dating.

Your children are different, and these differences will determine how easily they accept your dating and how quickly they accept your dates. Boys will react differently from girls, toddlers will react differently from adolescents, and grown children may just be impossible. Thinking out the potential problems

in advance will help you to deal more effectively with your
children once you begin to date. This is one situation in which
acting on instinct can only spell disaster.

What's Gender Got to Do with It?

"Daughters will identify with the mother and see her as a role
model," points out Dr. Victor Solomon. "Daughters of all ages
offer competition to the mother, from the little girl preening as
practice for one day attracting a man to the older daughter who
will compete on equal ground with her mother for the attention
of a man.

"Sons, on the other hand, relate to the mother, seeing her
as the model for the wife they hope to have someday. The son
may be threatened by a man in whom his mother shows an
interest, and even small acts of affection toward the man will
arouse a natural competitive instinct with the man. Handled
poorly by the mother, this competition for her can very well
threaten her son in his relationships with women when he grows
up."

"When I first began to date Phil, I told my fifteen-year-
old daughter where we went, what we did, almost everything,"
remembers Clare, a forty-three-year-old widow and the mother
of one daughter. "We giggled over the clothes that I chose,
over the way I fixed my hair, and over my dancing. I felt as if
I had suddenly become years younger and that my daughter
was a younger sister. Then all of a sudden, Annie drew back
and she would just change the subject when I started talking
about my social life. It seemed as if she was no longer interested.
I thought that she was just going through the normal ups and
downs of adolescence and I left it at that."

It was only after several months of near-icy silences between
the two that Clare realized that Annie was actually jealous of
her mother's dating. While Clare talked increasingly about her
social life and the fun that she was having, Annie was becoming
ever more aware of her own reclusiveness and exclusion from
social activities.

The problem had come about due to Clare's too-extensive
sharing of her social life with her daughter. As Dr. Steinfeld
asserts, "A single mother needs to try to keep a low profile and
not talk a lot about her dating. She must be sensitive to the

issues and remember that her daughter must be allowed to have her own growing up. You don't have to hide your dating from your daughter, but you should be private about your dating life. It isn't appropriate to share too much."

In the same way, mothers who are less than discreet with their sons regarding their dating life will also experience difficulty.

"Jeff was always a model student, then he suddenly stopped doing well on tests and his grades slipped," says Barbara, a forty-four-year-old mother of one son. "The divorce had occurred five years earlier, so I couldn't blame the change on that. Then I realized that I had recently begun a relationship that was more important to me than any of the others over the five years. I was so excited about my new interest, and I saw Jeff as being so grown up at the age of sixteen, that I had talked a lot about my new man.

"We had traded pointers on places to eat and generally laughed about romance at my age. Once I thought about that, I realized that all of my talk had stirred up jealous feelings in Jeff, who had put himself in the role of my protector for five years. Although I had dated various men in that time, I had rarely spoken of them, and Jeff knew only what he had seen when we had gone out as a threesome. My new interest had assumed a greater importance in my life. Jeff knew it, and he was jealous."

Although competition between mother and daughter might be more obvious when your child is an adolescent, even young daughters will feel the competitiveness with their mother. In this case, however, your daughter will be competing for attention with the man in your life rather than feel jealousy, as might the older daughter who has already established some sort of social life. Your little girl will want to share your makeup and your jewelry, and she will show off without any prompting when your date arrives.

Older daughters don't always compete for your man, although they might. Instead, they may experience feelings of envy when their mothers seem to be living a life that they see as being more appropriately theirs. A teenage girl who is never asked out on dates, who rarely goes to parties, and who doesn't have too many friends would naturally resent her mother's social life. Even the teenage girl who is moderately popular will feel jealous if her mother is out dancing every night and barraged by callers.

In some cases, single mothers have found that their teenage daughters actively compete for their men, either directly or indirectly. This is a highly uncomfortable situation for any mother, but it can be significantly worse if your daughter succeeds in snaring your man.

"I must have had my head in the sand," says Tricia, the thirty-eight-year-old divorced mother of nineteen-year-old June. "Sal is a year older than me and very athletic. You know the type. Tanned, slender, fit, and very youth conscious. I'm a tennis nut, and we played a pretty good game together. I've also kept myself in shape, and many people have mistaken me for June's sister. I thought that Sal and I had a very strong relationship.

"We dated for two or three months before he met June. Since she had her own life, I didn't feel that I had to make efforts to introduce them. Once they met, however, he pestered me with questions about her, under the guise of wanting to know more about my family life. My heart sank after a few days of this sudden interest, and I was flaming with jealousy that I kept to myself. Still, something that intense comes out in one way or another. I started to be 'bitchy' with both Sal and June, and everybody began to suffer.

"Then, as suddenly as it had begun, the questioning stopped. Sal, however, began to see less of me. He told me that his department was undergoing changes that required him to take home more work. June also began to change her habits. Instead of telling me when she had dates and talking about her latest boyfriend, she was silent. I thought that she may have been having romantic problems, and I tried to get her to talk. When she refused, I decided to let her alone.

"Well, I soon found out everything. Sal told me that he wanted to end our relationship. Then he really tore my heart out and told me that he had been seeing June for a month. They were in love, and he wanted to marry her and finish putting her through college. June had been afraid to face me, and she waited at his apartment while he told me.

"They have been married for eight months. I didn't, couldn't, go to their wedding. They had both betrayed me. We have started to talk a bit in the past month, and eventually we will have a cordial relationship. Losing my boyfriend to my daughter was the most painful experience that I have ever had, even worse than my divorce."

Both younger sons and older sons establish territorial rights over their mother and the intensity of their feelings may be astonishing. Although a toddler has little concept of the connection between men, women, and relationships, he does know that Mommy belongs to him because she reads to him, cares for him, cuddles him. Like his special blanket or his well-worn teddy bear, Mommy is a very important part of his life. She represents what is familiar and secure. When she begins to date, this feeling of security is threatened by someone, but his fears are much the same as those of a female toddler. It is the mother as his security and familiar object that he fears losing. He is not yet in competition over Mom with the men that she dates. He is just afraid of losing his protector.

Once he is eight years and older, a boy generally begins to see himself as "the man of the house," even if his mother doesn't encourage such behavior. As such, his mother becomes his responsibility to protect and to care for, in the absence of a husband. So when a new man enters his mother's life, he feels fiercely competitive, even if he isn't able to describe those feelings accurately. His feelings may be even more intense if his father has died.

"Stewart was seven when his father died," says Tina, a thirty-six-year-old widow. "At first, he would have tantrums whenever I went anywhere without him, even shopping with my sister. When I dated, I had to sneak out and meet my dates down the block. That was difficult, and I finally decided to be honest with him and tell him that I was dating, and I reassured him that no one would take me away from him.

"Things have gone fairly well, but this past year has been difficult. Stewart is now twelve, and he does everything around the house. I don't ask him to, because I believe that he should have fun and play. Still, every time I turn around, he's fixing something or suggesting something to make my life easier. The trouble is that he becomes angry if I ask any of the men that I date to help me. He feels that he is my protector and that the house is his responsibility. I love him, but I feel that he is cheating himself. I think it is time for us both to enter counseling before Stewart loses his whole childhood and I lose my social life."

How Does Age Change Your Child's Outlook?

In general, children under eight years of age have an easier time accepting their mother dating than do children above that age.

"I began to date eight months after my husband's death," recalls Nadia, twenty-five, the mother of a five-year-old son. "Simon still remembered his father and missed him, and I was frightened to tell him that I would be going out with a man for fear that he would accuse me of betraying his father. So I lied for the first date. I dressed up and told Simon that I was going to a business-connected dinner, a story that he believed since he had no reason to believe otherwise. Then I met my date downstairs and we drove off. When I returned after midnight, Simon was peacefully asleep, and the baby-sitter told me that he had played happily all evening. I wondered how he would have reacted had he met my date and if he knew that I was out having fun.

"I had the chance to find out a week later when I went out with the same man, and I decided to have him pick me up at the apartment. Simon was carefully prepared for the meeting. I told him as much as I could about Dave, and I answered all of his questions. In addition, I told him where we expected to be going and how late I would be home. He took in all of this information and nodded wisely, and I breathed a sigh of relief.

"When the doorbell rang, however, Simon headed for his room and waited until we had seated ourselves in the living room before coming out. He then came out and played the role of host by shaking hands as he sized up my date. I was both bursting with pride over my wonderful son and holding my breath for fear that he might say something out of line.

"He did make one point clear with Dave. As we were about to leave, after the sitter arrived, Simon looked up at Dave with his big eyes and, solemnly shaking his hand, said, 'Please take good care of my mommy.' I almost canceled the date then and there."

Over the age of eight, children become more strongly identified with their sex, and they begin to notice more, becoming more critical with what displeases them. As Dr. Marge Steinfeld has observed among adolescents in her practice, "Mom's dating adds stimulation to the lives of older children as they are beginning to experience the development of their own sexuality. Girls will feel that their mothers are competing with them, while boys will feel that the role that they often assume as the 'protector' is very much threatened by the new men in their mother's life."

Young children and teenagers may need careful management if they are to accept their mother's dating without seeing it as too much of a threat. Surprising as it may seem, older children, particularly adults, have a very hard time in this area.

Part of the problem is that older children have had a longer time of living with the parental relationship. In addition, they are generally more opinionated and more judgmental than younger children. To counter the criticism and disapproval of older children, you must be open with them without going into detail about the relationship. You also have to let your children know that the man is important to you and that you want to spend time together without the interference of others.

"I never thought that my two married children would kick up this much fuss over my going out with Jed," says Emily, a sixty-three-year-old widow and the mother of a forty-one-year-old daughter and a thirty-eight-year-old son. "They've both been divorced and remarried. You would think that they could apply a little of their 1980s morality to their mother. Not those two. As soon as I mentioned in passing to Sally that I had to find a special dress for a social function to which Jed was taking me, she bombarded me with questions. I guess that I didn't answer them to her satisfaction, because Allan called that same evening to ask me what was going on.

"What was going on? After six years as a widow, I have finally found the courage to try romance again, and Jed is the perfect romantic. I don't plan on embarrassing them with any wild escapades, and I will be available to them as always. The difference is that I now have places to go and people to see with Jed, instead of waiting for my children to give me a call or to invite me out. There is a whole wonderful world waiting for me."

The reentry may be a little difficult for Emily's children, but they will come to tolerate if not understand their mother's right to romance and happiness. Children of single mothers need to be reassured of their mother's continued affection and concern for them, but they must also be made to understand that their mother has a right to a social life.

Although the child of every age, toddler through middle age, may feel very flattered to hear his mother say "My children are my life," such devotion can become a burden as a single mother grows older. Children who once used every trick available to keep their mothers from dating may come to regret such actions in later years when they have lives of their own to pursue.

Is There Any Solution?

At this point, you may be wondering if you can do anything to alleviate the fears and doubts of your children and still enjoy an active social life.

The answer to this problem seems to lie in using discretion in your relationships.

One of the ways in which you can defuse a child's anger or fears about your dating is to introduce him or her to your date before you leave. Hiding a relationship and lying to your child can only increase his or her confusion once the truth is uncovered. This approach can be beneficial if you are dating one or two men over a period of time, and your children might meet them several times in that period. If, however, you are dating a number of men, it is better that you refrain from the introductions and that you meet your dates outside of your home.

Meeting too many men, all of whom seem to be important in your life, can also be confusing to a child. It can also be unsettling when the men are only one-date partners and your child never sees them again.

Once your child has met your date, keep signs of affection out of your child's sight until all of you are well acquainted. If you are dating someone over a period of time and your child has come to accept the man and to know the man well, then holding hands, a kiss, hugging, and other signs of affection will be no problem. If, however, you are just beginning to date someone or if you are dating several men, then such signs of affection will only confuse your child.

No matter what the ages of your children, you can have a warm and rich relationship with them and enjoy a rewarding romantic relationship.

Rather than view your reentry into a social life as being unfair to your children, and instead of suffering guilt because of your dating, you should feel good about yourself. Maintaining a social life will make your life happier now, and your children will find that their lives will also be happier when their mother is romantically involved, sexually satisfied, and feels good about herself.

13

Your Place or Mine—or Neither?

"Sex? You've got to be kidding," laughs Ariel, a forty-two-year-old widow with two teenage daughters. "My girls are usually home when I return from a date, so spontaneity is out at my place. If my date and I want to be intimate, it has to be at his place or at some neutral site. Most often, it is at some neutral site, because the widowers that I date have their children living with them, and even the divorced daddies who may take me out on weekends usually have their children staying over. Spontaneity in sex is out for me these days, and planning is in."

What's a single mother to do?

Child development experts agree that unless you are in a committed relationship with a man, sneaking a man into your bedroom for a few hours or having him sleep over is not a good idea if your children are still young and living with you.

Even if your children are adolescents or teenagers, bringing home casual partners is still not a good idea unless you endorse such behavior by your children. Keep in mind that your actions present a model and that your children will do as you do and not as you say.

Even if your relationship is long-term and your children are comfortable with the man, you should exercise caution and keep your sexual activity as it should be—private. You may have to opt for his place or some neutral site, such as a motel or a friend's apartment, if you want to enjoy sexual intimacy without creating future difficulties in your children's development.

Even if your children are grown and live away from home, you will find that your sexual relationships will create discomfort for them. They in turn will create discomfort for you, if you allow them that liberty.

Does all of this agonizing cast a pall over what should be the joyous topic of sexual pleasure? That isn't the intent. Sex should be fun, and it should be pleasurable. For the single mother, however, it must also be discreet.

Your Sexual Pleasure and Live-at-Home Children

You've got to consider your children when you decide upon your sexual policies, advise experts. Flaunting sexual activity doesn't prepare a child for life. Neither will sneaking around provide a solution. Children are more aware of everything that goes on in their homes than we realize. Certainly, your sexual arrangements must be made with great care and concern and attention to the values that you are teaching your children.

Women who choose to have a number of lovers may desire to bring them home as a matter of convenience, as well as in the mistaken belief that their home somehow puts a seal of approval on the one-night stand. Single mothers who chance such activity when their children are present are taking a big risk that may have unfavorable consequences in the future.

If you have younger children, you may think that it would be so convenient for you and your lover of the moment to just drive to your home, pay the baby-sitter, then settle down into your nice, cozy bed. You may even feel that this would be best for your children, even if they have never met the man, because at least you would be right in the home with them.

They don't even have to know what is going on, you may reason, because you will have the bedroom door locked and the television on to muffle any sounds of lovemaking. Later, when you are certain that they are still soundly asleep, you can sneak your lover out before anyone awakens. Perfect scenario, isn't it?

Not really. Never has the cliché "Little pitchers have big ears" been more appropriate than in the matter of the single mother's sexual trysts. Young children do not always sleep through the night. Even the youngest of children may be very aware that Mommy has a strange man in her bedroom and that there are strange sounds emerging from that room while he is there. Your three-year-old son should be asleep at two in the morning, but unaccounted-for sounds may awaken him.

Try as you may, you cannot be certain that your tryst will go unnoticed. The sad aspect of this situation is that your child may be too frightened either to get out of bed or to call for you. Instead, he or she may lie in bed, listening and building up a distorted and frightening vision of what is going on in your bedroom.

The danger of such trysts, to even the youngest of children, lies in their long-term effect on the child's perceptions of sex.

"There is no 'safe age' for a child when it comes to an awareness of the single mother's sexual activity," states Dr. Solomon. "Children begin gathering impressions and perceptions at very early ages, and such impressions are retained forever in the memory. Through hypnosis, memories have been evoked that date back to the age of one year and even six months. Thus, saying that your child is too young to know what is going on when you close that bedroom door is a poor defense. Even at the age of two, although the child may not have an intellectual understanding of sex, he does take mental notes. A distortion of impressions occurs at this age and his mother's moans of pleasure may be perceived as moans of pain. Thus, the two-year-old will come to associate the bedroom with pain. This is a very unhealthy experience for a child, and a difficult legacy for adulthood."

Sexual activity can be disturbing to your child if you are dating a number of men or even one man. However, seeing a continuous parade of men through your bedroom compounds the difficulties for your child.

"If you are dating a number of men, you should keep them out of sight of your children of every age," counsels Dr. Marge Steinfeld. "Even if you are dating one man, you should keep a check on your behavior and refrain from behavior that may be sexually stimulating to your children. Intimate touching and embracing that has sexual overtones are inappropriate in front of your children. And it is not appropriate for them to see you in bed with your lovers. Discretion should be your guide in determining how to carry on your romantic relationships in your home."

Adolescents are not as susceptible to the distortion of impressions that plague the younger child, but they will be influenced strongly by your behavior with men. Overt sexual behavior with the men that you bring home and promiscuity are not appropriate modeling behaviors for children. Further, as Dr. Steinfeld, whose practice has focused a great deal of attention on adolescents, has observed, such behavior will be sexually stimulating to adolescents who are already dealing with the problems of their own emerging sexuality. Why make their lives more difficult by flaunting your sexuality in front of them?

Even with a long-term commitment, you should exercise discretion in your sexual behavior. When a long-term relationship exists, and your children have become comfortable with a man, only then should you consider having him sleep over. When his frequent presence in your home has become natural to your children, then his staying overnight becomes part of the total relationship, and your children will accept it more easily.

Even in such situations when a long-standing relationship exists, and everyone can greet each other at breakfast without embarrassment or resentment, you should still be sexually discreet. Your adolescents may very much know what will happen once the bedroom door is locked, but there is no benefit in displaying your activities for all to hear and to see.

"Children tend to have false ideas about sex at all ages," points out Dr. Sharma Goodman. "You can be honest with your children when you have someone sleep over, and convey the feeling that there is nothing wrong with sex, nothing 'dirty,' but that you and your partner do deserve privacy. What you do with that privacy is your business."

Your Sexual Pleasure and Grown Children

"I love my children, but I'm not going to let them tell me what is moral and what is immoral at my age," asserts Vanda, seventy-four, a widow. "My son came over early on Sunday morning, without calling first, and he surprised both Seth and me and himself when he found that I was not alone in my bed.

"After sputtering for a few minutes that my behavior was a disgrace, my forty-six-year-old son tried to make me promise that I wouldn't 'embarrass" him anymore by having Seth stay overnight. 'What will the neighbors think when they see this man's car in your driveway all night?' he asked me petulantly. I believe that I shocked him when I informed him that several of the other widows and widowers on the block have done the same over the years. There is no advantage to making a permanent arrangement now, but we do deserve to enjoy the pleasure of each other's company.

"Oh, I could tell that he was just feeling a little jealous that I had another man in my life, aside from him, but I am a grown woman, and I'll do what I want!"

Grown children can place a different sort of restraint on your sexual life than young children who live at home, but their needs, although different, may be just as great as those of younger children. One important way in which you can alleviate their fears and their concerns is to exercise discretion in your sexual behavior. Yes, the same caution that is recommended in relation to young children.

Why do grown children often take such an interest in, and react so negatively to, the sexual relationships of their mothers? You may be surprised to learn that their behavior often stems from and duplicates the reactions of teenage sons and daughters.

Grown sons instinctively become protective of their mothers, who are most often middle-aged or older, when a divorce or death occurs. They set themselves up as the protector of their single mother and act accordingly in all appropriate situations. A single mother may actually encourage such protective behavior in her son because she feels comforted in having someone to help her and to guide her through the crisis period.

Later, patterns of reliance may develop, and the role of the grown son becomes stronger as he continues to "protect" his mother and to oversee her affairs. Therefore, even if he has a family of his own, it comes as a real shock for him to learn that his mother is reaching out to another man for fulfillment.

Although his rational self will recognize that it is only appropriate that his mother develop a rich and intimate relationship with a man of her own age, his emotional self rebels. He feels hurt, used, abandoned, and resentful, no matter how old he may be. He is afraid of losing his important position in his mother's life.

The mother's lover is a true threat to the grown son. Moreover, having to acknowledge that his mother may be having a sexual relationship is even more difficult than it may seem. In part, such reluctance of the grown man to accept his mother as a sexual being stems from the inability of all children to believe that their parents are sexual beings: "My parents never did that. They couldn't have!"

That doesn't necessarily mean that the grown child who has difficulty accepting his mother's sexuality is immature. He may be simply living out a life that is an accumulation of impressions, feelings, and accepted behavior. He has always viewed her as Mother, and his father's wife, and that view is deeply ingrained in his consciousness. Changing that view takes a great deal of effort.

The reluctance of the grown child to accept his mother as a sexual being is further complicated by the mistaken view held by society that older men and women must be asexual. Although the Gray Panthers and other advocates for older Americans have made changing this stereotype a part of their agenda, there is still a strong feeling among most people that sex is for the young.

Grown daughters operate on a different wavelength than the grown son, but their resistance to viewing the older single mother as a sexual being is equal to that of the son. If a daughter is married, she may focus her disapproval on the moral appropriateness of the situation and protest that her mother shouldn't be flaunting her affairs.

"My daughter pulled out all stops in trying to rearrange my life when I started to emerge from that year of mourning after my husband died," recalls Sarah, sixty-seven. "When I told her that I had begun to date Jeremy, she warned me that I have an image to uphold. She also warned me to remember Dad and to not 'dirty' his image. As if that weren't enough, she threw in the grandchildren for good measure, reminding me to remain the 'respectable' grandmother."

The grown daughter may also believe quite strongly that women of a certain age, specifically her mother's age, should not be sexually involved with anyone. This view may merely reflect the prevailing view of society toward the elderly and sexuality, or it may grow out of a resentment based on her personal situation.

"I had the hardest time making my forty-seven-year-old daughter understand that my sex life was none of her business," explains Tessie, a sixty-eight-year-old widow with two children. "She told me that it was disgraceful that we carried on as we did. This criticism came about because she had seen us walking with our arms around each other. That's nothing. The real carrying on occurs behind closed doors!

"Every time that she and I talked, my daughter would manage to bring up my romance with Mack and criticize my behavior. I finally sat her down and had a long talk with her about my life. When we started having it out, Toni confessed that she was actually jealous of me because I was having such a rich and active sex life as a widow and at the age of sixty-eight. Her marriage, on the other hand, had been without sex for over a year. Her husband was totally disinterested in sex, although their relationship had previously been good, and she was blaming herself. She took my suggestion that she talk honestly with him and see that he had a physical examination to determine if a physical problem was at fault. Their problem has since been cleared up—and my daughter no longer harasses me about my romance."

Unmarried daughters may also criticize their single mothers strenuously because they are jealous of their social lives. This is especially true of daughters who are in the age range in which available men are scarce. Seeing her mother romantically thriving and sexually active is hard for a socially and sexually unfulfilled daughter to accept. The unmarried grown daughter may try to make her mother feel guilty and immoral in the effort to compensate for her own lack of social success.

"She rarely called before Jim and I began dating," recalls Erma about her daughter. "Once she knew that I was going out with him frequently, and when she began to suspect that he was staying over some nights, my thirty-seven-year-old divorced daughter made me a regular cause.

"I'd receive calls at all hours. If I tried to cut the call short because something needed to be done, she would accuse me of not caring about my family and of being selfish. Then I would feel guilty and I'd hang on to listen to her moan about her unhappy social life, or the problems that her children were giving or her ornery boss.

"I wasted a lot of time by just marking time on the phone, and I soon realized that I was doing my daughter no good by indulging her. So I plucked up my courage and told her one evening that she'd be better off if she would stop calling me so frequently. Instead, I suggested that she make herself over, go out and socialize. She hung up on me and didn't call back for a week. When she did call, it was to thank me and to apologize. She is finally growing up and letting me live my own life. I promise to do the same for her."

Your Place, His Place, or Neither?

Where will you conduct your rarely spontaneous sexual relationship, without doing harm to your image, your reputation, or your children? Anywhere, answer single mothers. Anywhere, that is, where your children and his children are not.

Don't let the previous warnings about being careful about sexual intimacy in your home make you rule out that site, especially if your children are of school age. If you can't be spontaneous, you most certainly can be creative.

"Between his two children and my three, we thought that we would never have the chance to make love," sighs Elena, a forty-three-year-old widow who is dating a forty-seven-year-old widower. "Although all of our children are teenagers, we could never be sure that everybody would be out on a date at the same time, and the mercurial nature of their romantic lives meant that one child was bound to come home early and disgruntled. We never knew what to expect, so we didn't chance heading to the bedroom for the first three months that we dated.

"Not that we didn't try other arrangements. No-tell motels were out because those within our price range that offered 'day rates' were too sleazy, and the others were too expensive for more than an occasional session. A friend once gave Larry the keys to his beach house, but it was December and we found that the water, lights, and heat had been turned off. So we turned around and headed for home.

"We were just about considering dropping our standards and checking into a three-hour motel within our price range when the brilliant idea hit us. All of our children were in school full-time and that meant at least six hours per day that our homes were free. Of course, we both worked, but that was no problem. We decided to call in sick on the same day, and we spent a relaxed and glorious five hours in bed, just enjoying our freedom and each other. Naturally, we still locked the bedroom door, just in case, and left ourselves an hour to remove the signs of our lovemaking—make the bed, throw out the wine bottles, put fresh towels in the bathroom, et cetera."

If your children are in school full time, you can have your lover over during the day. If you have preschool children, if your children are not in school, or if either or both of you cannot take time off from your jobs, then your home is out unless you have developed a long-term relationship.

What about his home? If your lover is never-married and lives alone, then your sexual relationship can be enjoyed uninterrupted in his home. You may not like the inconvenience of having to pull yourself out of a warm bed at three in the morning to get home to your children, and your lover may grumble about driving you home, but that is a small penalty to pay for worry-free sexual intimacy.

If your lover is a widower, you will most likely be caught in the situation that Elena faced with both homes well guarded by children. If your children are school age, you can sneak in occasional days of lovemaking. But what do you do if neither home will afford you privacy to carry on your sexual relationship?

"It's not the ideal, but even a no-frills motel for regular lovemaking is better than no sex at all," says Sally, the twenty-eight-year-old mother of two preschool boys. "The man that I'm currently seeing has to be at work early, so we can only go out on weekends, and his daughters stay with him each weekend. Therefore, neither home is available. We've become good at concentrating on the activity at hand when we go to the day-rate motel up the highway. It's almost comical when I think of how often we've been there. The desk clerk already knows us as Saturday night regulars, and he hands us the key to the same room each week."

Would that work for you? If it seems to be an unlikely situation, if you can't comfortably overlook the flashing "day rate" sign outside the window, then you will have to be even more creative in your choices.

Couples who have found the motel to be their only choice, and whose budgets don't permit more than the no-frills version, try to vary their site occasionally. They like the security of one motel for their "regular" times together, but they also enjoy splurging occasionally for a night at a more upscale site.

"Once a month or so, we check into an elegant motel and splurge—champagne and the works," laughs Sally. "It's like taking a vacation, for a few hours. We can enjoy all of the luxuries that our no-frills motel lacks. That break from the ordinary also encourages us to be adventurous in bed and to try something just a little bit different each time."

These options work well when you and your lover know each other well enough to decide what will work and what won't. When a single mother starts a relationship with a single father that she has just met or has met only recently, she may soon learn that the home of the divorced father may not always be a good option.

Most single mothers are very much aware of the presence of their children, thus making them usually more cautious regarding sexual activity in their homes. Divorced fathers with visitation rights, on the other hand, are more likely to overlook this responsibility because attention to the effect of their relationships on their children is not necessarily a full-time concern. As a result, single mothers who have sexual relationships with these men may be in for some unpleasant surprises.

"The music played softly in the background while candles flickered on the side tables," recalls Brit, a thirty-nine-year-old divorced mother of two. "The wine had given the already perfect evening a rosy glow that washed over me as we embraced tightly on the overstuffed sofa in his apartment. For the first time in months, I was feeling totally female. My children were safely at their grandmother's, and I was here in Kurt's luxurious apartment, playing out a role from some romantic movie, or at least some popular 'soap.'

"Then I heard the soft voice call, 'Daddy, you frightened me. I didn't know that you had come home,' and I turned to see a slight, pajama-clad figure in the doorway. She had been watching us necking and petting on the sofa. I was humiliated, and I felt sorry for that young girl, who looked to be about seven years old. Kurt couldn't understand my upset and he told me that she was used to him bringing his dates home.

"That was it for me. Not only didn't he have the good sense to warn me that his child was in the house, but he didn't seem to realize that seeing her father and an anonymous woman groping on the sofa could be upsetting to his daughter.

"I was also upset to be lumped together with all of the other 'dates' that he had brought home and that his daughter had seen. So I ended that evening immediately by switching on a nearby lamp, introducing myself calmly to his daughter, and calling a cab."

You may have some difficulty in scheduling your trysts if you are involved with a divorced, widowed, or never-married man, but the task is monumental if you persist in a relationship with a married man. The married lover will give you the most difficulty of all, report single mothers who have juggled clandestine romantic relationships with married men. Doesn't that make you want to think more than twice about such relationships?

Although you may have the same problems as you would in other relationships with men who have children, because you certainly can't go to their homes and the presence of your children may make your home impossible, married men have additional disadvantages. Even if your home is free during the day because your children are in school, a married lover will probably be afraid to come to your home in broad daylight for fear that someone might recognize him or his car. Part of the problem can be solved by putting the car in your garage and ignoring the curious questions of neighbors, but the fear of being recognized remains.

What can you do? Single mothers have found that such relationships are destined for motels that are out of the immediate area or for "borrowed" apartments or beach houses. If the prospect of having to meet in this manner appears sordid, then you might want to steer clear of the married man.

"I know that he's married and I don't care," says Melanie, a forty-six-year-old widow with one teenager. "It's not my job to police his marriage. For all I know, his wife may even know and maybe she doesn't want to rock the boat. Anyway, I like what we have right now, and I just want to enjoy him any time that we possibly can get together.

"It's hard because Barry is well known in this town and he would be easily recognized if he came to my home during the day while my son is in school. Even the local motels are dangerous because he is recognizable. That has forced us to drive about seventy miles to the beach house that his father left him. It's rustic and very cold in the winter, but our lovemaking heats it up. I may get tired of this someday, but not right now. He makes me feel so wonderful when I'm in his arms."

Sleepovers and Live-Ins

"It was late on a Saturday night and the roads were icy, so I suggested that Dale stay over at my house," recalls Allison, a thirty-three-year-old widow with three children. "My children were five, six, and seven then, and they had never seen Dale even go near my bedroom, let alone sleep with me, although we had been dating for eight months. We decided that we wouldn't use this night as an excuse for forcing the sexual part of our relationship on them.

"To avoid any unpleasant surprises for the children, Dale slept on the couch that night. When the children awoke the next morning, they climbed all over Dale, and after we untangled the bodies, we all enjoyed a big breakfast. Then the kids dragged Dale outside and they played in the snow.

"The day went fast, and soon it was night again and time to decide what to do about Dale. The children had gotten to know him very well in the eight months that we had dated, and they always looked forward to seeing him. My oldest son, Jake, waited until supper was over, then he shyly asked Dale if he would stay the night again. The other two clamored for Dale to say yes, and he looked to me for approval. When I nodded, he looked at them and said very seriously, 'I'd like to stay, but that couch is very bumpy. I can't sleep very well on it.' My guys had the perfect solution. They shouted out, 'Sleep with Mommy. Her bed is comfortable, and it's big. There'll be plenty of room.'

"We followed their advice, but we listened all night for the sounds of restless children at our door. There were no sounds. My children slept all through the night and woke up cheerful in the morning. They liked the idea of having Dale sleep in my bed.

"I think that I should tell you that, from the first night, we did make it clear that we should have privacy when the door was closed. That helped us to be more comfortable in being sexually intimate several nights later. It has been three months since the kids first suggested the 'sleepover,' and there have been no scenes. By the way, Dale and I will be getting married next month."

Don't count on being as fortunate as Allison and Dale. Your children will probably not suggest that you invite your lover to sleep in your room or to move in with you, although they might. It is more likely that you will have to make the suggestion to your children. As Dr. Steinfeld has found, "When the relationship is long-term and the kids are familiar with the man, then it will seem natural for him to sleep with you as part of the total relationship."

Don't confuse your familiarity with a man for closeness between your lover and your children. You may have been dating him for six months and going to his apartment for much of that time. While you may be very familiar with him, your children may still view your lover as a relative stranger. Even worse, they may see him as a usurper if he tries to move in without having first invested some time and effort in making himself a familiar member of the household.

No matter how much you want to bring your lover and your children together under one roof to become one happy family, be cautious that you don't move too quickly for everyone's comfort. One of the most tempting mistakes that you will face is your premature effort to bring about "instant intimacy" between your children and your man. Your lover may also have a strong desire to form a family unit with you and your children, and he may try too hard. This may turn your children completely off to the idea.

Rather than force the situation, take a more leisurely route to the change of living arrangements. Speak honestly with your lover and ask him to spend some free time alone with your children, talking after dinner, playing games, or walking together. Let them build up a relationship that is separate from the relationship that includes you. In this way, you can test the waters and determine if your family can comfortably accommodate a new member, and if you are willing to give up the exclusive relationship that you have with your children.

Surprising as it may seem at this moment, you may find that you will become jealous of your man if your children become too close with him and if he is welcomed too readily by them into your home. Consider in advance if you want to share them with another adult. If you don't, don't ruin what may be a perfectly good relationship as it stands.

Once you know your heart, then you can decide if you want to encourage your children and your man to become close. If you decide that you want this, then help him to become accepted. The better that he comes to know your children and the more familiar that they are with him, the better are the chances that they will welcome him into the household.

Don't expect too much of the situation. Even the most valiant effort may not succeed in swaying the mind and heart of a stubborn child who is determined not to let another man move into his father's role. Your children not only need but they deserve patience in becoming accustomed to the idea. They will eventually have to accept your decision, but life will be easier for everyone if they grow to want to accept the decision. You should help them to realize that by adding your romantic partner to your household, you are enriching what already exists and not detracting from it.

14

Sexy—and Celibate

"Celibacy? Are you kidding?" laughs Rena with disbelief. "That's a choice that went out with the Dark Ages. No woman today would consider celibacy as a reasonable way to handle her sex life. The only woman who is willingly celibate is either someone who has dedicated her life to religious service or the woman who can't attract a man no matter how hard she tries."

Wrong. Celibacy is an option that many formerly married women have consciously chosen because they want to refrain from sexual activity, not because they have to.

Not all women are as contemptuous of the concept as Rena. Many formerly married women have found that, for one reason or another, they experience a lessened sex drive after their divorce or the death of their husbands. At the same time, however, their energy levels in other areas increase. This is one benefit worth considering, but that alone is not reason enough. Rather, celibacy for at least a time can make good sense because it allows you to stand back from the world and to examine your priorities.

Sexual relationships require an emotional investment that many single mothers can't afford to make without short-changing other areas of their lives. Even if you function well professionally, maintain stable family relationships, and give your children needed quality time, you may find that there is little time left for yourself. How, then, do you fit in the added dimension of a sexual relationship?

A more important question may be, "Do you want to fit in a sexual relationship at this time, or are you under the mistaken impression that you have to?" Yes, *have* to.

Although the sexual revolution has cooled somewhat, society has remained performance-oriented in regard to sex. Single mothers, however, are damned if they do and damned if they don't. Too active a sexual life will elicit disapproval from some, be they family, friends, or your children's schoolmates, while no sexual life will start people wondering out loud if you are "normal."

The decision to seek out sexual relationships or to refrain for a time while you get your life in order should not be made with such outside views in mind. Make your decision based on your own priorities.

Some single mothers feel that everything else in their life seems to run smoothly—their children are happier, their jobs are more challenging, their car runs better—when they have an active and satisfying sexual relationship. If the same is true for you, if a sexual relationship is a priority in your life, then celibacy need not be considered.

If, however, you find that you rarely have free time to spend with your children and that you never have any time to spend alone, you may not be willing to expend even the minimal time required by a sexual relationship. If you crave the time to enjoy a warm bubble bath more than you crave the time to enjoy a warm male body, don't feel that you have to forgo the former and seek out the latter—unless you want to.

It isn't unusual for a single mother to become involved in a sexual relationship in an attempt to gain sorely missed adult companionship. Loneliness, fear of the future, the desire for emotional closeness, and the need to be part of a couple again, if only in bed, lead women who have no desire for sex into sexual relationships. Sex becomes the currency that buys companionship and attention. Conducted in this way, a sexual relationship is demeaned and so are the people involved.

You don't have to trade in this manner. If you want to refrain from sexual involvement and still have adult companions and people with whom you can be emotionally close, this is the time to begin cultivating friendships. Other mothers, your family, your children, and male friends, both straight and gay, can be sources of companionship, emotional closeness, comfort, and attention.

Whatever your reason for choosing celibacy, for however long, you can rest assured that you have much more company than you realize.

As Dr. Victor Solomon suggests, "Celibacy is a choice, and it is a choice that women have long been making. Many women who have been widowed choose to remain celibate as they raise their children. With the threat of AIDS today, celibacy is a choice that makes sense. It's funny, with all of the resistance to celibacy for the unmarried, many people overlook the fact that there may well be more celibacy in marriage."

What Do You Mean—Celibate?

Tell someone that you are celibate, and you will not only be faced with a look of disbelief, but people are often not sure that what you have just admitted is true. In a society so sex-obsessed as our own, to deliberately refrain from sexual activity is decidedly odd unless your conviction is linked with a religious or cult effort. To admit to doing so is even more odd.

What does celibacy actually mean? In its most general sense, to be celibate means that you have made a deliberate and conscious decision to refrain from sexual activity. Of course, you may also consider yourself celibate if you have been sexually inactive through no choice of your own but only because of circumstances. Making the conscious decision seems to provide a greater feeling of strength and control over the lives of those single mothers who choose this route.

"I don't hate men, nor do I hate sex," protests Andrea, the divorced thirty-three-year-old mother of two preschool daughters. "My daughters are having a difficult time understanding why their father left, and so am I, and we have a lot of healing to do together.

"Sex to me is very important, and I enjoyed that aspect of my marriage very much, but I also know that I would become intensely involved with any man with whom I was sexually intimate. I don't have the energy, nor do I want to spend the time now to enjoy that kind of involvement. When life has quieted down again, then I will take the time to think about sex. For now, I am enjoying the relative tranquility of celibacy."

Andrea is attractive and young, and she could easily have a sexual relationship with any one of a dozen men who have asked her for dates in the past year. She dresses well, but not in a seductive manner.

"No need advertising if you won't deliver," she reasons. Since her divorce a year ago, she has dated several men who find her choice of celibacy hard to believe. This is especially so because she is divorced and the stereotype of the divorcée appears to persist.

"One of my dates tried to steer me into bed and wouldn't take no for an answer," she recalls, still troubled by the memory. "Just making the decision to be celibate was not reason enough for him to simply accept my decision without being annoyed or feeling rejected. He cajoled me, humored me, teased me. When I still refused to begin a sexual relationship with him, he threw out that old standby, 'What's wrong with you? Don't you like men?' I like men, all right, but I hate his type."

Why Choose Celibacy?

"Celibacy is a good idea for me now and in my present life," says Fern, the thirty-two-year-old mother of a preschool son and a seven-year-old daughter. "My divorce was final nearly two years ago, and I have dated in that time, but I want to date on my own terms. Look, I love to dance, to laugh, to have fun. I also like men, very much.

"Sex, to me, is not something that you engage in like a game of tennis or cards. I want to really share myself, body and spirit, with a man whom I respect and care for. I also want to know that he respects and cares about me. Who wants to be just another piece of meat to be picked up at a singles bar, or to be bought with dinner and a show?"

The view taken by Fern is often voiced by other women of all ages who have chosen to remain celibate, for at least a time. Celibacy is a choice, just like having a sexual relationship with a man should also be a choice. Unfortunately, the view generally taken by society often works against the woman's right to choose a sexual relationship or to pass.

How often have you viewed celibacy as a choice? Don't be surprised if this is the first time that the concept has ever been presented to you in this manner. The usual choices that are offered to women, and that often appear in guidebooks for single mothers, tend to focus on when to begin a sexual relationship, not whether to do so. Refraining from sexual activity is considered unnatural, a crime against your rights as a human being and as a woman.

But what about the feelings of a woman who is expected to pay a man back for dinner and the show by going to bed with him? Isn't that a crime against a woman's human rights? Do you just stop going out on individual dates and instead go out with groups in which everyone pays her own way?

That's one option. Another option is to keep a firm hold on your self-image and realize that a man asks you out because he wants to spend time with you. If he takes you dancing, to dinner, to a show, whatever, it is his choice to do so.

You in turn have the responsibility to be good company and to enjoy yourself with him. You should also plan on returning the favor in the future with theater tickets or the like, if you want to keep it friendly. Nowhere is there an agreement on your part that, in order to pay him back for spending money on you, you will return the favor with sex at the end of the evening. Still, the unspoken expectation usually does exist in the mind of the man and in the minds of many single mothers.

At the least, even if you are not celibate, such an assumption by a man is very inconsiderate. As a single mother, you can't just invite him into your home at the end of an evening and make payment in kind. Nor are you treating your baby-sitter fairly if you go to his place and extend the evening by two hours. Since the issue of sex doesn't usually come up until near the end of the evening, as a single mother, you are pretty much at a disadvantage anyway in determining your options.

If you are celibate, and if you want to remain celibate, then you will just have to brave telling your date when he broaches the subject. The only comfort is that this may be the only time that you will have to tell him. A man whose only interest in you is sexual will not bother calling again. On the other hand, a man who wants more of you and who enjoys your company will not need to be told again.

How Do You Stand It?

Single mothers who have chosen celibacy usually keep their decision to themselves until they have to explain why they have no interest at the present in beginning a sexual relationship. If you should make the choice, you will find that explaining to your sexually active friends your reasons for being celibate and the manner in which you handle your celibate state will become a full-time job.

Women who have never been without a sexual partner for any amount of time will question how you can bear to refrain from both sexual activity and from the physical closeness of a man. Others will bless themselves silently and thank their lucky stars that they haven't become like you.

You see, celibacy is very much considered a curse among sexually active women who cannot bear the thought of going without a man for more than a night or two. Women who may vehemently criticize you for your conviction are usually dependent individuals who need to have someone, anyone, in their lives. The quality of the relationship, their feelings of self-worth, and their own satisfaction with life are not issues that they consider.

How do you stand it? The question is of little consequence if you have made the conscious decision to remain celibate. Many women have found that they become highly creative in other areas once they channel their sexual energies in other ways.

"I have become a human dynamo," says Arlene, the thirty-seven-year-old widowed mother of a teenage daughter. "The sexual drive and the sexual energy that I had when I was married were powerful. In retrospect, I realize that sex devoured much of my free time and most of my attention. For the time being, I am channeling that energy and drive into building up this small company so that my daughter and I will have security in the future. When I have gotten where I want to be, then I can relax and enjoy my natural sexuality once again. Of course, then I will have to shift gears again and lessen the intensity with which I approach work.

"In the meantime, my celibate state beats the daylights out of the men that ask me out. I have a good figure and wear my clothes well. In addition, I still flirt and joke with men as I used to. Old habits die hard. The difference is that I now enjoy my dates more because I am not waiting for the dessert of sexual activity after a date. The event is the date itself. When I'm ready for a sexual relationship, I'll let the right men know in no uncertain terms."

In the interim, many single mothers, like Arlene, who have rechanneled their sexual energies, find that male friends, both straight and gay, help them to maintain their social lives. Sex may not be of interest for the time being, but men still remain attractive.

If you have never known a man who could be your friend, someone with whom you can have dinner, see a movie or play with, or just talk to, now is the time to discover this special pleasure. You may have to share him with a lover or wife who may barely tolerate your relationship, but your time together will be worth making any compromises.

Male friends who truly care about you will provide the emotional closeness, companionship, and attention that you need, but none of the sexual hassles if you desire to remain celibate. In the right circumstances, a straight male friend can offer the added benefit of becoming your tender and intimate lover once you have decided that celibacy is no longer appropriate for you.

Substitutes and supports are fine, but what does a single mother do when she is sexually aroused, and she is celibate either by choice or situation?

"I think of my ex-husband and the late support payments," jokes Verna, a forty-two-year-old divorced mother of three. "No, seriously, I concentrate on something that really needs my attention. It becomes a matter of mind over body for me. I can sometimes *will* my body to no longer feel a need for sex. At other times, the need is so intense that I have to do something physical, like housework or exercise or take a walk, to drive the feeling away."

Does this surprise you? Did you think that making the decision to remain celibate, or being in a situation that has made you celibate, would mean an end to all sexual thoughts and arousal? That is hardly the case. Most celibate single mothers find that their sexual fantasies and sexual needs remain as strong as ever. The difference is that the means of releasing sexual tension have changed.

"I may be celibate, but my sexual feelings aren't dead," says Jean, a thirty-nine-year-old widow with one son. "My husband and I had a wonderful sex life and I miss that very much, but I'm not ready to start a relationship with any man right now. When I become sexually aroused, I don't try to drive the feeling away. Instead, I retire to the privacy of my bedroom and I satisfy myself sexually. I masturbate. It's not a lonely and furtive act, but a pleasurable experience. Of course, sex with a man is always better, but it has to be the right man."

How do celibate single mothers cope with celibacy? They choose to place sexual relationships in perspective and to cultivate other areas of their lives until they are ready to enjoy and nurture a sexual relationship. They may wait until the right man comes along, or they may wait for the right time. In any case, until they are ready to begin a sexual relationship, celibacy presents them with a viable alternative to random sexual involvement.

Just This Once—Please

Most men who date a single mother who has decided to remain celibate for a time view her as a challenge to their masculinity. Those who take her decision seriously will try to get her to change her mind for them, while others see her decision as being only an act that is designed to excite their interest. Still others don't care about her decision because sex at the end of the evening is expected, both as payment for the money spent and as a boost to the man's ego.

"It's too bad that many men consider their sexual prowess and skill to be their total worth," says Ellen, the forty-four-year-old mother of two sons. "More than one man that I've dated has been crushed because I wouldn't go to bed with him no matter how much he may have badgered or cajoled me.

"It's not as if I haven't been sexually active. I certainly have, and now I'm 'resting' for a time. Right after my husband left me, I did what many divorced women do. I went out and forgot my troubles with a series of forgettable men.

"After that sexual binge, I felt a need to purge my spirit. There had been too many men in too short a space of time, and I felt used and old. In my own way, I have viewed these last six months of celibacy as a chance for renewal. There has been no sexual frustration because I made the decision for myself, and I don't resent it. This is coming from a woman who had sex with her husband every day and sometimes twice a day during the sixteen years of our marriage. What can I say? It was good, but the marriage fell apart anyway. And celibacy is also good, for me, for now."

What should you do when a man insists on sexual activity despite your intent of remaining celibate? Assuming that you are not with a near stranger that you've met only hours earlier at a bar and who could be carrying a weapon, you should stand your ground.

Of course, even sexually active women should have the right to refuse a date's demands for sex. You have to eliminate from your thinking the mistaken belief that dating and male-female relationships must include some sort of barter system. He takes you out and buys you dinner and you give in to sex. That's the wrong way to go about it. Rather, whatever occurs at the end of an evening should be desired by you both and enjoyed by you both. It should not be a service rendered.

"What I did was a little extreme," admits Janet, the forty-four-year-old divorced mother of a daughter. "I was sick of fending off groping hands and countering men who protested that I couldn't really be celibate. Some men, especially newly separated and divorced men, are fanatical about scoring. Every date is another notch, or they view the night as wasted. Some never-married men and widowers have the same attitude.

"I've made several rules for myself since I've been single. The main rule is that I never take home or go home with a man that I've just met that evening. An equally important rule is that I always carry adequate cab fare and my checkbook. However, I can talk up a storm before giving them my telephone number for future contact. One man that I met talked with me for a whole evening, then asked me out for dinner for the next. I accepted, and I felt more comfortable than I had for a long while because we had already talked about my being celibate.

"The dinner was pleasant and our conversation was lively. After dinner, we strolled through the outdoor gardens of the restaurant and talked. He held my hand, and I felt nicely and innocently romantic. As we came to a large tree in the restaurant courtyard, he kissed me passionately, then told me, 'I knew all of that business about celibacy was just a game. Wait until we get to my place tonight. You'll be talking differently.' I protested, but he brushed my protests aside.

"I'm not a gambler, but I do believe that you have to know when to bluff, so I bluffed. Pleading the need to visit the 'powder room,' I told him that I would meet him at the entrance to the courtyard. Once in the restaurant, I called a cab. Then I hurriedly wrote out a check to him for the cost of my dinner and my half of the tip. As the cab pulled up, I handed the check and a brief note to the maître d' and asked that it be delivered to the gentleman who was waiting by the courtyard entrance.

"True, I ran away, but my instincts had warned me that I would have been in a very difficult position with him had I stayed. I had tried a firm stance, and I had tried to refute his remarks. Nothing had worked, and I doubt that I would have succeeded any better once we were alone.

"One more note—that check has not been cashed."

The issue of how to fend off the unwanted sexual advances of a date who is determined to save you from celibacy is very much the same issue as that of the sexually active woman who wants to choose the men with whom she has sexual relations. Just because you are sexually intimate with some of your dates doesn't mean that you are the same with all. Although not the specific topic in this chapter, the issue of your sexual rights underlies the whole book, and so does the question of choice.

When the Time Is Right

The time to become sexually active may come after a few months of celibacy or after a few years. How long you remain celibate depends upon the quality of your life, the intensity of your family relationships and friendships, and why you decided to become celibate.

Do you remember Miriam's lesson in Chapter 1 of this book? She started out by dating, at the request of family, then dropped the frantic social schedule and settled into enjoying a life that was based upon group activities with her children and their friends and other activities with her coworkers. After several years of mingling with other parents, some of whom were single fathers, Miriam met and married a man who had become a deep and trusted friend and whose children were friends of her own. In the years preceding, however, she had not dated and she had remained celibate.

How long might you be celibate? How long do you want to be celibate? More important, how long will it be until a relationship comes along that will make you want to give yourself totally—your mind, your heart, and your body?

Unless you have decided in advance how long you intend to remain celibate, and few women do unless they are making celibacy a part of an overall regimen or way of life, you will probably make a spontaneous emotional decision to leave celibacy and to begin a sexual relationship.

A variety of reasons influence a woman's decision to become celibate. When those reasons are no longer valid, the celibate state is often no longer valid.

Single mothers who use celibacy as a means of distancing themselves from intimacy in order to organize their lives along other lines frequently find that the desire for an intimate sexual relationship becomes a priority once their lives are stable. Once they can relax and turn their attention to enjoying life, sexual pleasure is welcome once more. Not only must a woman feel that she has the available time and the capacity to enjoy sex before she will leave celibacy behind, but she must also be convinced that she has the energy to invest in a sexual relationship.

For many single mothers, celibacy functions in a more complicated role. The sexual relationship is often the most intense interaction of a husband and a wife. When the marriage ends due to death or divorce, the sexual relationship is also ended. For a woman who has been deeply hurt by a divorce and who still grieves for her husband, a sexual relationship represents her marriage and all that it meant to her.

Like the widow who feels that she can never love anyone else but her late husband, the deeply grieving divorced woman may also feel that she can never love anyone else but her former husband. To make certain that she keeps that vow, she may choose to remain celibate rather than to be "unfaithful" to her true love. It really doesn't matter if her divorce has been bitter or if her husband has remarried. A woman who sees herself as still married will turn to celibacy in order to be the faithful wife.

Is this healthy? No, say experts who see this manner of "choosing" celibacy as being, in essence, a forced choice. A divorced mother's celibate state may help her over the rough spots in the early months after her separation from her husband and the divorce, and that's fine. If she continues to mourn the lost marriage, and if she remains celibate as a symbol of her mourning, then a wise move would be to seek counseling that will help her to put her grieving into perspective. After she has recognized the intensity of her grief and learned how she has been misusing celibacy, then she can make a choice to either remain celibate or to seek out sexual relationships.

The widowed mother who is mourning the actual death of her husband may turn to celibacy in the same way to maintain her fidelity to the marriage. There is a period of mourning, individual with each woman, that must be worked through. Continuing to be the wife emotionally is important to that role. However, such grieving should not be permitted to continue for too long.

"I don't believe in suffering," asserts Dr. Shdema Goodman. "If the grieving process after death or divorce continues for too long a time, then a woman should enter therapy. She needs to strengthen herself and to gain the inner strength and self-knowledge that will permit her to get on with her life."

Because the decision to become celibate is in itself a commitment and not only a one-night decision, the decision to leave the celibate state should be similarly well considered. Being attracted to a man who also finds you attractive will start you reconsidering your celibate state, but you will probably give the move a little thought before actually beginning a sexual relationship with him. If you have remained celibate for several months, you will find that the time will have given you a different and clearer perspective on the nature of male-female relationships. You may have a better idea of the type of man that you want to meet and to mate with, and you will definitely have a more favorable perception of yourself.

Thus, when you feel that celibacy has served its purpose in your life, you will leave that state behind with no regrets in order to begin a satisfying and fulfilling relationship on your own terms.

You will know when that relationship is right and that the time is right for it in your heart, your body, and your mind.

15

When Should You Make a Commitment?

"Don't make any big personal decisions for a year after your divorce or the death of your husband," recommend single mothers, both divorced and widowed. "Don't sell your house, don't get married, don't move in with someone, and don't have anyone move in with you. Don't make any decision that will tie you into a long legal battle should you decide to change your mind."

Single mothers who move too quickly to marry or move in with someone often find that the fear of being alone has led them to make a hasty marriage or merger. In the process, they not only limit their own lives, but they may put severe restraints on their children's lives. When you make such a move less than a year after the divorce or death, you are not allowing enough time for healing to occur. You are still vulnerable. Your children are still vulnerable. What you may think of as your salvation may quickly turn into a hell, for you and your children.

Is It Time for Commitment?

The time to make a commitment can be any time that you feel ready to stop looking around for romance because you have found the man that you want. Who you are will determine how long the commitment will last, and if it is even a commitment at all.

What do you mean by a "commitment"? That's an important question for single mothers to answer honestly, before they promise anyone else their heart and their time. Deciding in advance what you expect in a "commitment" can save substantially on hurt feelings, dashed hopes, and destroyed dreams.

Does commitment mean that your partner will date you exclusively and that you are expected to do the same?

Does commitment mean only that every Saturday night will be free for that one man, with the rest of your nights—and his—going to other partners?

Does commitment mean that your children become involved to the extent that they will begin to view your man as their surrogate father?

Does commitment mean that you will retain separate residences?

Does commitment mean that you must live together?

Or does commitment mean marriage with all of the trimmings?

If you don't know what you expect from a "commitment," then you had better give it some thought in the context of your current family situation. Just as important, you should make certain that your partner is sure of what he wants, and that each of you knows what the other expects.

Love may be blind, but you cannot afford to be. The happiness of your children is at stake, in addition to your own future.

Is Marriage the *Only* Choice?

You don't have to look toward marriage as the only means of making a commitment. There are other possibilities.

Once you have selected one man, out of the many that you have met since your divorce or the death of your husband, it's time to decide what to do about your relationship. If neither of you wants to date others, and if you have both determined that this is it, then you have already made a commitment. The next step is to decide what you will do about it.

If you are a single mother with young children, you may very well choose to remain unmarried until your children are off to college or married. If this is the case, then you may be fully willing to take a chance on a long-term relationship that is headed for marriage—but in a decade or more.

The men that you meet may or may not agree with your decision, and that alone serves the purpose of separating the suitable men from the unsuitable. When you meet a man that you find attractive, appealing, and sexy, you may want to narrow the field down to just you two. At the same time, you may want the freedom to raise your children alone and in your own way. What can you do?

You will find that men do exist who may want the same freedoms as you, who are also willing to make a romantic commitment. A divorced father who has custody of his children may want to raise his own children without competition from anyone else in his home. A widowed father may feel the same way. Both of these men will want a woman in their lives, and they will probably feel better if that woman is someone who will become close with them and their children but who will not impose her presence or will on their household. Your thoughts, exactly.

Divorced fathers who do not have custody of their children may also have a reason for wanting a committed relationship that doesn't include living with a single mother or raising her children. Because he is a "weekend daddy," his life and home must change from Friday to Monday, then back again. While many people can make stepfamily situations work and even thrive, others prefer not to risk a marriage in the experiment. So they opt for raising their children alone and then marrying when the children are grown.

A noncustodial father may have an additional reason for not wanting to raise your children with you and in the same house. He may be feeling a strong sense of guilt because he left his family and his children are being raised by someone else. To play the role of daddy to your children would increase his guilt feelings over his children.

When two people who want to raise their children alone meet and mate, the benefits to their children and to themselves can be substantial. You can make a commitment, yet still retain separate residences and separate lives. Your affectional ties will thrive even if you don't want to marry. For some of us, the social milieu, the presence of our children, and other factors make us decide that living with a man without being married would not work well. We don't, however, want to marry. Thus, we resort to separate residences.

Separate residences are not only important in "keeping up appearances," but they may also be chosen by single parents who do not want constraints on their freedoms. Stop and think before you protest that having children is, in itself, a constraint. Remember that you and your children have developed a specific rhythm to your lives together. You may not always agree with each other, nor are your rules always followed. Nonetheless, you have pretty much come to know what to expect from each other. For the time being, you may want to keep your home life as it is.

The fear that their living space will be invaded also holds single mothers back from turning a commitment into a marriage or a living-together relationship. The man in your life may also be hesitant to combine living spaces unless he is currently residing in a furnished room.

Whether or not he has children, a mature man who has his own apartment or house has acquired material goods that have meaning for him. He may not want to share them with young children, even if he very much likes your young children. He may also be hesitant about crowding both residences into one. And it may not be financially possible to buy or to rent a larger home or apartment.

You may not agree that maintaining separate residences supports the idea of a romantic commitment, but you may still want to avoid marriage. Living together can provide you with full-time adult companionship and a genuine partner with whom to share the responsibilities of parenthood.

For widows, living together is a better choice than marriage because of the manner in which the Social Security laws are structured. If you are a widow with children and you remarry, you will lose your widow's benefits. You may argue that you will gain your new mate's income in its stead, but you can also benefit from this support if you live together. Further, although you should think positively, keep in mind that nearly two out of three remarriages with children fail. So act accordingly.

Choosing to live together is not as simple as just packing up your worldly goods or his worldly goods and moving to the same site. You are a single mother, and you must keep in mind that your children will be "living together," too. Not only must the household structure change because there will now be a mate in it for you, but your children will have to deal with another adult and another potential source of discipline.

The extent to which your live-in lover will be authorized to discipline your children, and you to discipline his, must be worked out in advance. This is very important, and we will discuss later in this chapter how your children fit into relationships of this type.

Marriage is another choice that you can make, and psychologists vary in their feelings as to how marriage will affect the family unit and particularly the children. Psychotherapist Dr. Marge Steinfeld suggests that the important issue is not whether you and a man marry. What is important is that you have a stable and committed relationship.

"A committed relationship is safer and more secure," says Dr. Steinfeld. "It may mean living together, and if that's your choice, then your children must be made aware that this is a decision that has been reached by two adults. Talk with your children regarding the how, when, and why of the situation. You have got to be considered a family and be identified as such."

Many of you might more easily agree with the views of clinical psychologist Dr. Victor Solomon, who says, "I believe, personally, that marriage is the ideal relationship." And you will establish your commitment accordingly.

You have several choices in determining the formal structure of your relationship, once you have decided to make a commitment. Whatever your choice, the needs of your children must be kept in the forefront of your thinking. You can begin by determining how involved your children are to be in a relationship before it becomes serious, so that you can make their role in the "committed" relationship that much easier.

How Do Your Children Fit In?

Single mothers who enjoy successful romances differ widely in their views as to how soon a child should be made a part of the romantic relationship. Some of you may prefer to keep your children entirely out of the relationship until a serious commitment to remain together has been made, while others may decide that the second date is the time for your children to join in the fun and for everyone to get to know each other. Your decision as to the right time to introduce your children into the relationship depends on the age of your children, your involvement in the role of mother, and the personal situation and personality of your partner in romance.

You have got to give a great deal of consideration to how your relationship does affect the feelings and concerns of your children. As Dr. Solomon suggests, "There must be no artificiality or phoniness. A man should not feel as if he has to please the child to please the mother. A child will know very quickly when a man is bartering time with the child to make the mother happy.

"A child is looking for quality. The younger child is looking for a man who comes up to the house and gives him a hug. The older child wants someone who will talk with him, not just pass time.

"The way in which the man relates to your children may be important in lessening the threat that he poses to your sons. The introduction of the man into the family must be gradual. Your son must first see the man as a nonthreatening male—kind, decent, playful, and relating to the boy almost on a primary level. In this way, the boy will feel good about the man as a person and he may easily accept his mother's relationship."

Rather than introduce your child into the relationship, you will be fairer to your child if you look at the situation from his perspective. The men that you date are being brought into an already established relationship between you and your child. Therefore, your child is actually suffering an intrusion into his neat little world of the home and mother. Older children as well as younger children experience such feelings of intrusion.

"The issue is one of a total relationship in which your child does play a significant role," says Dr. Steinfeld. "You must emphasize respect in your dealings with your children, both for their feelings and in their reactions to you. Children are not throwaways. Kids are your kids forever and what you do affects them profoundly."

So, how do you introduce your children into a relationship?

"I have always had my dates pick me up at our home," says Rhonda, the thirty-five-year-old divorced mother of one son.

"To make my son feel more assured about the evening, even when it was the first date with a man, I would have him meet the man at the door with me, and then we'd sit for a few minutes and talk. I was divorced when Danny was three years old and started dating the next year. The sitter has always been told to come a little later so that we could have that talk.

"Perhaps I have been too confident, but I've always laughingly warned dates in advance that my son would be 'checking them out,' so they were prepared. My encouragement of this ritual left a man no choice but to be a good sport and to go along with the situation. Had I asked them rather than told them, I might have met with resistance. As it was, every man that I dated was good-humored about it.

"Now, let me play 'expert' for a moment and tell you something else. I only dated about five or six men over these last three years, so Danny wasn't faced with a parade of men. I am selective, which has been good for me and for Danny. To be truthful, at the age of seven, he is a very confident and articulate little guy who benefited from meeting my dates and talking with them.

"I am now engaged to a man whom I have dated for the past year, and whom Danny has greeted and spoken with before most of those dates. They have built up a relationship because I introduced them at the start. As a result, there were no special preparations needed to tell Danny that we will be getting married. He's been expecting that for some time!"

The relaxed manner in which Rhonda has eased her son into all of her relationships from the start is a hard act to duplicate. Many men may balk at meeting your children, mainly because they may have little familiarity with the children of that age or with children at all. Other men might not have any affection toward children, and yours will be no exception. Still others will be intimidated by meeting your family if you have several children who may be adolescents. Your adolescents will probably not be cooperative, either. Therefore, before you try to bring everyone together at the outset, you have to play "What if?" in advance to determine if such a meeting is feasible.

A more common way in which the single mother involves her children in a relationship is to wait until a commitment of exclusivity has been made. In other words, when you and your partner agree that this is a romance and that you will date no others, it is time to introduce your children—and his.

How can you meet and greet each other with a minimum of hard feelings? Begin by choosing an activity that will be fun for the children and appropriate to their ages, but that will also allow for some time in which to interact with each other. This is an especially good rule if both you and your partner have young children or teenagers. However, you will have to do some rethinking if there is a great difference in age between the two sets of children.

Although you and your lover may be the same age, you may have married young and have children who are in their late teens. He may have married later and now have children who are preadolescent. The amusement park, the zoo, and even the county park will probably offer little in the way of joint amusement. That's another problem that we'll tackle later.

Once you have decided on an activity, talk with your lover and share all of the information that you can about each other's families. If he is never-married or otherwise childless, or if he has adult children who have their own families, then the responsibility is yours. Remind your lover of the ages of your children, and talk with him about what children of their age and your children in particular like to do. Try to tell him enough about each child to make each child stand out from the others.

If your son bats a ball like next week's draft choice, tell your lover so that he can be sure to suggest that they play a little baseball as they get to know each other.

If one of your children is a good swimmer, your lover can join her in the pool and use racing her to get through what may be a protective wall.

At the same time that you fill your lover in on the intimate details of your children's likes and dislikes, you should be telling your children as much as possible about him. In addition to letting them know the demographic information, make certain that you convey to them the fact that this man is important to you and that you want them to spend time together.

After all of your planning and preparing and worrying has been done, step back and let nature take its course. You can't step in and direct the action, however you might want to; you just have to leave it to fate.

If your children have had your relationship thrust upon them with little advance warning, they may be upset and they may want to get back at you. Or they may be jealous, and they may hope that negative behavior will end the relationship. Discuss these possibilities with your lover in advance.

Your lover and your children may not like each other at all, and they may both try to avoid each other in the future. Expect this, and don't worry too much about it. Eventually, there will be some coming together, if only because you are the connection between your lover and your children.

If they don't hit it off, try hard to stifle words that will blame either side. Instead, however much it may hurt, unless either side has been overtly cruel and hurtful, don't place the blame anywhere. In private and separate conversations with your lover and your children, explain how you feel about their failure to get along and point out reasons in the potential relationship and not in the individuals themselves for this lack of fellowship.

What if your children are grown? What if your children are much younger or older than his children? In either case, you will probably not have to worry about the way in which your children interact with his children because they will not see very much of each other. Yet it is still a good idea to bring the families together for a social gathering, if possible, so that everyone can at least meet everyone else. If you are going to make a commitment, then you want to share the good news with others, even with those who would rather not hear it.

The best type of gathering to permit such introductions is informal, either a barbecue in the yard or in the park, or a buffet dinner in your home. You and your lover should divide the responsibilities for instructions so that he will take care of his family and you will take care of yours. You will try to make certain that all your children meet his, and vice versa. "Mingle" should be the word of the day.

Once the introductions have been accomplished and your children are aware that you have made a commitment, it's time to decide what everyone's role will be in the newly reorganized family. If you are to be spending a lot of time together and if your children still live with you, then your lover will play an important role in their lives. Before all of you can begin living your roles, however, you have to be sure of what they are.

Who Is He, Anyway?

Your lover has to establish a role for himself with the assistance of everyone involved in your new unit. There are many questions to answer if the relationship is to be successful.

- How much time should you and your lover spend alone?
- How much time should your children and your lover spend alone?
- How much time should the new family unit (you, your lover, and your children) spend together?
- How does your lover become an "insider" to the family?
- Can he, should he, discipline a child who misbehaves?
- What financial obligations does he accrue for your children?
- How do your children view him in relation to their father?

All of these questions are important for you to answer to make your "commitment" a success, and to determine the way in which your relationship is to evolve. If your commitment is marriage, then the answers to these questions should reflect the formulation of the new and formal family unit. There are clearer guidelines in that case, although disagreement will still arise in regard to discipline, financial obligation, and trust.

Of particular importance in determining how your lover or new husband fits into the family is the issue of how much disciplinary power he is granted over your children.

Dr. Marge Steinfeld states, "The mother should stay in charge of her children until a 'commitment' is made. The man should not assume the parenting role until the adult relationship has solidified. Even then, you will have to trust a man a great deal to give him responsibility over your children."

"The one rule that I always stood by when I dated someone and my children were present is that I am responsible for their behavior and I would discipline them," states Darlene, a forty-five-year-old widow with two children who has remarried. "Even when Tom and I decided upon exclusivity in the relationship, we each took responsibility for our own children. Taking that route simplifies the situation. Besides, they are my children, and I should have the main authority over them.

"Since we've been married, however, Tom and I have functioned as a unit. Therefore, we are the authority over all five children. Privately, we have agreed that each of us will take the responsibility for playing the villain with our own children. This has been so effective an act that his kids have often come to me to protest his harshness, and my kids have gone to him with the same complaint.

"We've found that splitting the discipline along those lines prevents a lot of hard feelings for both the children and the adults."

The live-in lover remains marginal unless he, too, has rights in the relationship. Although you may not want to give him disciplinary rights over your children, you have to permit him some means of guaranteeing his rights in the household. Some sort of reporting system with punishment dealt out later, or another form of disciplinary system should exist. Like it or not, even if you have chosen not to marry, you have formed a stepfamily situation just by choosing to live together. This new structure demands that certain principles of behavior that are common to all families should exist.

You can't make your children respect your lover, but you can insist that they follow certain "rules of the house." To follow them, they have to be told what these rules are, and that is your job.

You and your lover must also determine what his financial obligations will be in the new household. You and he may have decided that he will assume all household costs. Or you may have decided to split all costs down the middle. Another choice that single mothers make is to split all household and food costs evenly, but each person is responsible for his or her own additional expenses. As a single mother, this means that you have to meet all of your children's expenses. Give that a little thought.

If you are divorced, you may have child support to count on, and there are survivors' benefits if you are a widow. These, however, are not riches, and you will have to consider where you will obtain the money for household expenses.

"Those few months had me climbing the walls with expenses," recalls Phyllis, the thirty-eight-year-old divorced mother of two. "I agreed that Jason and I would split the cost of the rent, heat, and food down the middle, and that each of us would pick up our own additional expenses. That seemed fair enough at first until I realized that he has a better job than I do, so he makes more money. In addition, while my salary was fine to run my old apartment, adding him and his many possessions to our family unit meant that we had to move to a bigger place. Stupidly, I agreed to rent a house which cost a lot to heat, and the rent was very high.

"I struggled to make up my half of the obligation and to pay my children's expenses. With no child support coming in, that is really difficult. Naturally, I soon fell behind on my half of the payments, but Jason was a doll and made up the difference for several months. Very soon after I started to fall behind, however, I noticed that he was really becoming harsh with my children. We had agreed that I would keep them in line, but he had begun to order them around and to punish them. I talked with him about it privately and he told me flatly that as long as I wasn't pulling my weight financially, he was in charge in the home.

"It seems that this had been coming for a while, but I just hadn't seen it. The more I had gotten into financial debt with Jason, the more dependent I became and the greater were his rights. We ended the live-in relationship soon after that discussion, and I moved with my children into an apartment again. I will never get into a relationship like that again. If I'm going to live with a man on an everyday basis, I might as well get married!"

Single mothers who have chosen to remarry find that their new husbands must also establish their authority in the home, but many women still prefer to retain control in disciplining their own children.

"I know that it isn't right, because Beau has rights in this house, too," says Carla, a newly remarried former widow with three children. "Still, it hurts me every time that he tells one of my babies what to do, or where to put things, or how to act. The other day, I couldn't help but tell him that he was way out of line in telling my baby boy that he couldn't go with his friends because of the disrespectful way in which he talked to me. Children can be like that, and Beau still hasn't learned that."

Carla's "babies" are fifteen, seventeen, and eighteen, and the "baby" that talked back to her was her seventeen-year-old son. It appears as if Beau has quite a few bad years ahead of him until the children are grown and out of the house.

Making a commitment requires that you create a structure within which the new family that is formed can function effectively. At the start, you are the connection between your romantic partner and your children, and the greatest pressure will be placed on you. Both may be pulling at you, demanding attention and requiring that they be heard first. You may feel emotionally torn apart.

How can you ignore your children while you tend to the needs of the romantic relationship and your lover? On the other hand, is it fair that you ignore the relationship and your lover at the insistent demands of your children?

Before further problems erupt, you will have to establish your priorities and let everyone know where you stand. Most mothers have no hard-and-fast rules as to whose needs must be met first. As one divorced mother said, "I sometimes just tell everyone that I'm retiring from the situation and they can sort it out themselves. I have needs, too!"

Whether the choice is separate residences, living together, or marriage, you and your children will experience a change in the rhythms that have developed in your life together. Introducing a man, your lover or new husband, into the family circle can be painful at first. It will be even more difficult if he, too, has children. Yet if you plan in advance and work with your children to help them see that they are not being excluded, you will have an easier period of transition.

16

How Do Your Children Feel?

"I want my mother to date and have a good time because she deserves to have fun," says Robby, nine, an only child whose parents separated when he was fourteen months old. "I really don't think that kids should try to tell their mothers when to date or not to date, or who to go with. But if she's thinking of getting married again, then I think all three of us should talk about it.

"I wouldn't mind if she got married, because then I'd have a father, and I'd like that. He'd have to discipline me because he takes that responsibility when he marries a woman who has a child, but that's O.K. What I would mind is if they had a child. It's O.K. if he has children that would live with us because then his kids would have only one real parent, him, and I would have only one real parent, my mother. But if they had more children together, then I'd be jealous. That baby would have two real parents in the house."

Many children express an ambivalence similar to Robby's regarding their mothers' dating. They truly want their mothers to enjoy a social life, contrary to what you might expect, but they worry about how they fit into that social life. They also worry about the consequences.

"If she gets close to a man, I worry if the man will like me or just my mother," adds Robby. "I wonder 'Do I want a father?' 'Will she have another kid?' 'Will she still have time for me?' I also wonder if a man who would marry my mother would

175

feel like an outsider and worry about fitting in with us. I guess that you just have to talk about it."

Few children are as articulate as Robby about their fears, but the children of single mothers all have fears. They worry about everything. About losing their mothers. About gaining a father. About having to move. About having others move in. About not being wanted anymore. About fitting in.

Why Do We Have to Be Different?

Logic will get you nowhere, neither will government statistics do the trick, with a child who is convinced that being the child of a single mother is "weird." You won't gain favor by pointing out that over 12 million children in this nation live with their divorced, widowed, or never-married mothers. Nor will you make any headway by reading off a list of the children in his school whose parents have divorced and whose mothers now carry the ball.

When the notice from school reads "Bring your mother and father," when the handmade art project/Christmas card has a mimeographed insert that reads "Dear Dad and Mom," or when the school persists in sponsoring a "Father and Son Breakfast," you may also begin to believe that your life is "weird." The truth is that the two-parent family is still the norm despite rising divorce rates, increased numbers of never-married mothers, and the higher visibility of the single mother.

Your child might feel right at home in an urban school in which a large number of the children are either living alone with single mothers, or with single mothers and their current lovers. If you live at some distance from metropolitan areas, the balance will be different and you will probably be one among only a few single-mother families.

If this isn't "weird" enough, your specific situation may make life even harder for your child.

"I've been telling everyone that my father died when I was really small," relates Kevin, the ten-year-old son of a never-married mother. "We moved here three years ago, and I already knew that my parents never were married, but I was ashamed so I lied. My mom found out, and she cried that afternoon and hugged me for about an hour. But it's all right because she does all of the things that both fathers and mothers do. Nobody here would understand about it, so I just lie."

In addition to his "lies," Kevin also daydreams sometimes that he will meet his father and that he could then say "My parents . . ." like most of the other children in his class. Other times, he gently prods his mother to marry so that he could have a "dad" like the other kids.

Life in a small town has left its mark on him.

What most single mothers don't realize, but what most of their children already know, is that there is a hierarchy of "weird" operating here.

Thanks to the media coverage of rising, falling, and stabilizing divorce rates, being raised by a single mother as the result of divorce is the "norm." Any other reason for having only a mother to raise you can create a lot of questions for a child.

The widowed mother, once a small-town fixture in movie Westerns, has come to be regarded as something of an oddity by many adults as well as children. Children born during the time that our country was engaged in the Vietnam conflict can credibly claim that their fathers died in battle. Today, there are children as young as twelve who did lose fathers in that manner.

For most children today, however, the claim that their fathers have died and that their mothers are widows is sometimes disputed by cruel and bullying children in their school.

"I had to fight him because he said that I was lying 'bout my father being dead," protests seven-year-old Jimmy, who was one year old when his father died in a car crash. "I had a father once, but this kid kept laughing and telling me that I'm a liar. He said, 'Admit it. You're mother ain't been married.' I just hit him and ran home."

The stigma of "unwed" motherhood is a dandy insult to throw around in the right social milieu, but it carries little importance in the urban area in which this type of single motherhood may very well be the most common. In such areas, the two-parent family is the oddity. However, you do not hear anyone hurling insults about having two parents in the home.

Being different is not the only problem that the children of single mothers face. Once their situation has been cleared up for their classmates and other friends, your child can proceed just like any other child in making friends, squabbling over petty nonsense, and having fun. They will usually make no issue of their family situation until they are reminded of it by a school notice of activity—or by your behavior. School notices can be ignored or shrugged off, but the single mother who seems to be going out of her way to attract notice can be a problem.

You may be doing nothing more than dating, but this alone can make you stand out in a way that may have your adolescent blushing. Although children may agree that their single mothers should date, they are not so positive when faced with this reality.

How Children of the
Single Mother View Dating

"Jimmy's older sister dates because she's in high school," points out Sandi, the very grown-up ten-year-old daughter of a thirty-six-year-old divorced mother. "My other friends' brothers and sisters date, too, but they're all young. But my mom! It is so uncool to have the older brothers and sisters of the kids you hang out with see your mother walk into a movie holding hands with some guy. I mean, who can face them? You know?"

The "guy" to whom Sandi refers is her mother's lover of three months and someone of whom Sandi personally approves. It is the public aspect of her mother's dating that makes her uncomfortable. There is also an edge of jealousy to Sandi's protests about her mother dating, because dating, to her, is for the young, i.e., the high school crowd.

Although this perception is a little shaky, it does point up to the possibility that she probably feels that her mother isn't acting as she expects a mother to act. Rather than staying home and performing domestic duties, Sandi's mother is doing the same as her friends' brothers and sisters. And although Sandi is still too young to date, her mother is offering her competition in the bargain.

Preadolescent girls are not the only children who experience jealousy when their mothers date. For some, the sight of a mother who changes from weekday weary to Saturday night pizzazz can be a bit unsettling.

"When it's Saturday night and my mom is all dressed up to go out with Ed, she looks like a model," coos Laurie, the four-year-old daughter of Pat, who is twenty-five and divorced.

"She has on her big earrings and her dress is so pretty. I try on perfume and I smell good like she does. Sometimes, I ask her to stay home 'cause I miss her. But I like Megan my babysitter, too."

Laurie is a big-eyed and precocious child who is fascinated by the transformation of her mother each Saturday night. After a little more talk, Laurie admits that she feels jealous of her mother's boyfriend, and she sometimes wants to tell him that she hates him. She never will because she knows that her mother will punish her. Another fear that Laurie has each time that her mother goes out is that she might never return.

"My daddy left us when I was a baby and he sometimes writes to me," Laurie informs her listener. "I never see him. I only have my mommy. And I'm afraid that she'll leave, too. Sometimes I'm afraid that she will go away with Ed and never come back. That's why I try to act really good before she goes out."

Young children may protest against their mother's dating for several reasons. They may echo Laurie's fear of having their mothers leave and never return after a date. Because of this, your young child may cling to you as you get ready to leave or cry to go with you. This desire to tag along is voiced with the aim of keeping you safe from the unknown evils that steal parents away. It always serves as a warning to you that your child is afraid of losing his or her security—you.

A second reason for your young child's resistance to your dating may be jealousy. It may be jealousy of the man with whom you are spending the evening, or it may be jealousy of your ability to leave the child with a sitter and go out to have fun. Some children view their mother's dating as proof of their own inadequacy, and they view their mother's social life without them as evidence that their mothers find them boring.

"I wish that my mom could have fun with me," complains eight-year-old Billy, whose mother, Lisa, thirty-two and widowed, goes out each Friday and Saturday night. "Whenever I want to play a game with her at night or sit down to talk about something, she never has the time. She is always tired because she works all day. Why can't she talk to me on Friday night instead of going out? She works all day then, but she isn't too tired to go out. I'm only a kid, but I am her kid. Why doesn't she want to have fun with me?"

Billy makes a very important point that many children of single mothers frequently voice. If you work all week, you may be too tired to be a ready listener in the evening when your children want to talk about their day at school. You may not even have the time to just curl up and gossip with them.

Between making meals, getting clothes ready, balancing the books, and getting the house straightened for yet another day, your schedule may leave little down time. Your children may grudgingly understand your limited time and take their troubles somewhere else. At the same time, they find it hard to accept that your busy schedule that so often excludes them contains time to date on Fridays and Saturdays. Placed in their position, you would also find such behavior insulting and perhaps frightening.

You can make life a lot less threatening for your child, and also lessen the resistance to your dating, if you would take the time to view your dating from your child's perspective. Would you like to be pushed aside each evening by a mother who is too tired from a day at work, yet who has the energy to go out dancing Friday night after an equally long day at work? Might you not feel offended and worthless?

If you have lost one person that you love, a parent, wouldn't you be fearful of losing your remaining parent every time that the two of you were apart?

If you were an adolescent or a teenager, wouldn't you be embarrassed by a mother who dressed in the extremes of fashion and who acted like a lovestruck teenager in front of your friends?

Are you beginning to see why children of all ages have objections when their single mothers date?

There are ways in which you can alleviate your children's anxiety, but doing so will take time. It may very well take as much time as dating every Friday or Saturday night. However, if you can spare that time, you should be willing to offer your children as much.

Billy's mother is thoughtless in turning her son aside all week with the excuse of being too tired to spend time with him in the evenings. Perhaps Fridays are slower days for her at work, and perhaps she really isn't as tired at the end of that workday. Even if that is true, would you believe it if you were Billy?

The key to lessening Billy's anxiety lies in helping him to realize that he is important to his mother's life, but only she can do this. Lisa has to decide that, however tired she may be, there will be shared activities and time alone that she can enjoy with Billy every day. He may be happy to help her get dinner ready, or he can do his reading homework in the kitchen as she cooks. Perhaps they can plan to do something offbeat for dinner one night each week. Later in the evening, Lisa can relax while they listen to story tapes, read together, or just talk. These activities don't require a lot of energy, but they do exhibit a lot of love on the part of the single mother for her child.

Laurie's resistance to her mother's dating can also be lessened, but her mother will have to provide Laurie with more assurance that she will return after every date. To an adult, the fact that Pat has come home after every date so far may be assurance enough. It isn't enough for a child. Laurie's anxiety would be lessened if she could have something tangible to reassure her. As Laurie tells everyone, she really likes the nights that her mother goes out because the combination of the special perfume and jewelry make the evening seem special. Lurking in the background are those horrible fears of abandonment.

Pat might find that Laurie will be less anxious if she makes her nights out also special for her daughter. She can tell Laurie that while she is out with Ed, Laurie can wear a very special piece of jewelry from her mother's jewel case. Pat can pick this out in advance to make certain that it will withstand the tugging of little fingers. She may also let Laurie dab on some perfume on those nights to add to the fun of the evening. As the evenings become special for Laurie, as she looks forward to them, her anxiety will gradually fade away.

So far so good. But how do you quell the anxiety of an adolescent who considers a dating mother to be the ultimate embarrassment? You may bridle at the suggestion, but you should be willing to bend a little to achieve peace in your home. Adults usually go to different places on their dates than teenagers, but sometimes you can't help but go to the same movie theater, the same restaurant, or the same athletic event as your children's friends. The mere fact that you are dating is embarrassing to your child, but he or she can handle this. It's your behavior with your date that will result in teasing.

Is it necessary to be so clingy and cuddly in public with your date, or can you wait until later to show your affection? Would you consider yourself a social outcast if you weren't dressed in the latest teenage fad, or would something less bizarre yet fashionable also suit you? Although the temptation is to forget that we are adults who can appreciate teenage fashions and behavior from a distance, it is better for our children that we remember our role and the image that goes with it.

Where Do I Fit In?

"My mother and I were on our own for six years," Allan proudly tells his listener. He is twelve, the oldest son of a thirty-six-year-old divorced mother. "I used to help my mother by carrying things in from the car and fixing little stuff around the house. We used to sit and read together in the evenings and she'd talk to me. That's gone forever, I guess.

"My mom has been dating Sam for about four months and he's always here now. She says that I can go and play basketball with the guys and try out for sports at school more than before because Sam will take care of fixing stuff. I think that she really just wants to get me out of the house now that she has Sam."

Allan has been displaced as the "man of the house" by Sam, and the demotion is painful to accept. For six years, Allan's mother had placed him in the position of protector, helper, and confidant. He played an important role in her life, and this role served as the way in which he defined himself in life. He was the eldest son, the all-around helpmate, and the substitute husband. When Sam more appropriately began to assume these duties, Allan felt as if he had been fired by his mother and without due cause.

Where does your child fit into your dating relationship? Children need security and stability, and they need to know that they have a definite niche in your life. Providing them with this assurance is no easy task.

- Telling your child "Of course, I love you, honey" is not enough to counter behavior that may be telling your child that you'd be happier if he were to get lost.
- Including your child on an outing or two with your lover, then announcing that you have made a "commitment," is not enough to make your child acquire the instant "family feeling" that you may desire.

• Exhibiting overly affectionate or sexually suggestive behavior with your lover in front of your child will not win his approval of either the relationship or of your lover.

Your children need to be told and shown that they occupy a place in your life and in your love that is invulnerable to time. Other people may enter your life and theirs, but these others are added to your lives. They do not take the place of anyone, especially not your children.

The Grown Child

Much of what has been said in this chapter focuses on the fears and attitudes of the younger child toward dating by the single mother. Problems appear most often in the younger age group because these children live with their mothers and they are more immediately affected by activities.

This does not mean that the grown child is without his own concerns when his mother dates. Rather, the concerns for grown children are different and sometimes more difficult to resolve because the grown child is often more judgmental and more opinionated than his younger counterpart. He has also lived in the parental relationship longer, and thus he has greater difficulty in accepting the change of seeing his mother out with other men.

"I just couldn't believe that my mother would be going out dancing with a man who is fifteen years her junior," exclaims a distinguished-looking forty-eight-year-old executive. "Look, she had me when she was only eighteen years old, so this guy is only three years older than me. She's sixty-six years old. Hasn't she got any sense?"

Ashton's mother is sixty-six years old, and she has got sense. The problem is that she also has a grown son who is afraid of losing his mother to a man who is not much older than himself. Their relationship creates serious doubts in his mind. It reminds him that he is indeed a man in middle age who might also be dating a woman of his mother's age had he not just remarried for the third time to a woman in her twenties!

The problem with this grown child is that he has not yet grown to the point that he can acknowledge and accept his age and maturity.

Elizabeth, Ashton's mother, was widowed when he was forty and just going through the celebrated midlife crisis. As he was leaving his first marriage, he found it comforting to slide into the role of the dutiful son who took over his mother's financial dealings and the decision making regarding her property. His business acumen made him a valuable resource in the early days of her widowhood, as well as a personal comfort. This role did not continue for too long because Ashton soon recovered from his first divorce and was remarried within weeks to a young woman who left him little time to play the dutiful son.

Her son now occupied once again, Elizabeth began to enjoy some of her inheritance. She took an extended cruise around the world and savored both the pleasures of travel and the delights of the men that she met on board. In the years that followed, she took other extended trips to Europe, Hawaii, and the Orient. In all of her travels, she was never without male companionship. Either she traveled with a man, or she met men in her travels and they continued on together. Some of her companions were significantly younger than she, and she has a storehouse of pleasurable memories of her trips that have nothing to do with landmarks.

Ashton, busy with his second marriage and family and embroiled in the business world, hardly spoke with his mother and he never worried about her. She was traveling and she seemed happy for the little time that they visited with each other. He certainly never suspected anything of her rich and varied sexual life.

At the age of forty-eight, with a third marriage in trouble and his mother involved with a man of his age, Ashton is very much interested in Elizabeth's activities. He needs her reassurance and support, and he's afraid that she won't have time to offer them to him. He is afraid of losing his mother's love and caring, but he protests that he is afraid that his mother will be "played for a fool," "taken for a ride," "used and then discarded." These clichés are spoken with an hysteria that exposes his own concern that Elizabeth won't be there when he needs her.

Should she remarry, and to this fifty-one-year-old man, where would he fit in? Ashton has considered the ridiculousness of a situation in which his mother's husband would technically be considered his "dad." He supposes that his mother must be having a sexual relationship, at her age, and he is upset by the thought. He is also upset by the thought that her lover, because he is only three years older than Ashton, would supplant him as the son in the family.

There is no age limit above which your children will fully accept your dating and romantic relationships. Younger children will worry about their own physical and emotional security because they realize their helplessness in dealing with the world if they should lose you. Your grown children may be afraid of losing their role as the protector, the helpmate, or even as the child. You can help your children of all ages to better accept your social life if you are open and honest with them. Surprises are what destroy their sense of equilibrium.

17

What Are the Feelings of Men Who Date Single Mothers?

"I think that one of the key issues in dating a single mother is that equal time be spent with the child, as well as with the mother," asserts Art, a swarthy and handsome thirty-seven-year-old navy lieutenant. Never-married, he has nonetheless dated a number of single mothers. "I have gone to playgrounds, amusement parks, movies, the beach, and on picnics with single mothers and their children.

"I think that a good mother wants to try to balance the time spent with her child and the time spent in dating. To me, a woman who wants to include her children in activities shows that she cares a lot about her children.

"Don't get me wrong. I do enjoy the time spent alone with a woman, but her children should not be ignored."

Not every man who dates single mothers has such respect for her children. The man who thinks in this way is quite a find. Still, this welcoming attitude doesn't and shouldn't mean that he should be manipulated. With such consideration for you and your children must, of necessity, come rules to keep the relationship running smoothly.

"For me, how a woman treats her children and how she disciplines them are very important," says Art. "Relationships that have worked the best for me have been those in which the

186

mother has continued to play the role of mother, i.e., teaching her children that there are limits, providing firm but kind discipline, providing her children with interested attention, and making certain that her children are fed well, clothed properly, and kept clean. These are basic, but some of the single mothers that I've encountered place such care at the bottom of their list of priorities.

"When children have a healthy respect for their mother's rights, then the romantic relationship can go more smoothly. Instead of worrying about a child walking in on you in bed, you can relax and enjoy each other if her child has been taught that a closed bedroom door means privacy. Instead of a scene at bedtime when both the lover and the child want to sleep in the mother's bed, the child will go to his own bed at the mother's request. In my relationships, I have seen that children who receive concerned guidance, care, and attention are more secure in their mother's love, and they feel less threatened by their mother's romance."

What Role Do They Play?

"To tell the truth, I make it a point to not play any role at all except that of lover," says Alan, forty-four and divorced. "When I ask a woman out, I don't ask her if she has children or if she doesn't have children. I feel that it's her responsibility to take care of the child-care arrangements, et cetera. The children are not a part of our romantic relationship, and I prefer that they remain in the background.

"The women that I date seem to agree with me because I have had several successful, long-term relationships with both divorced and widowed mothers in the two years since my divorce. One of the reasons that I like to date single mothers, if I have the choice, is that they know the score, and they realize that the male-female ratio is against them. That's why there has been no complaint about my attitude toward keeping their children out of the relationship. We really never have to go to her apartment since mine is totally free for sex."

Short, but not sweet. The attitude expressed by Alan is one that too many men have toward the single mother. It is also an attitude that many single mothers have of their lot in life, and it leads them to make compromises that are not necessary.

A man like Alan feels that he is doing single mothers a favor by asking them out. And he may be doing just that. After a single mother has been out with someone as unfeeling and, yes, as negative as Alan, many other men begin to look good in comparison.

Not all men cut themselves off so completely from a woman's children when they are involved in a relationship. Many men, however, have to be shown the way to interact with your children, and they have to be made aware of how important your children are to you. If you do not value your children, if you do not feel that they are integral to your life, then you may as well not waste a man's time in trying to convince him to bring your children into the romance.

"Playing the part of surrogate father is a pleasure to me," says Len, twenty-nine years old and never-married. "I have been in one relationship with a twenty-eight-year-old divorced mother for the past year, and her six-year-old son Eddie and I have had some good times. You know, you really can't remember what it feels like to pitch a ball, or just walk through the park as a kid, or any of the other things that kids do, unless you have a child along with you.

"He sees his father on Saturdays, so I know that I will never be his 'daddy.' That spot is reserved for someone else. I've gotten the more important title of 'friend.' He is a well-behaved child, and he loves and respects his mother. I also love and respect his mother. That is our strongest bond."

Men like Len can do much to enrich the life of little boys whose fathers are only part-time. In this case, Eddie's father is a gruff, boisterous man who booms rather than talks. Len, on the other hand, speaks in calm, well-modulated tones. Although some weeks it has been difficult for everyone, Len usually goes over to the house after Eddie has returned from his father's. After the initial confusion, Len's calming voice and presence are usually enough to bring Eddie back into the tranquility of his mother's home.

The question of discipline is a source of continued debate between single mothers and their dates. Many mothers maintain that no matter what, no matter the circumstance, their children are their children and it is the mother's role to discipline them. Many men would prefer that it be this way, but the problem is that single mothers don't always recognize when discipline is needed.

"Unless a situation really got out of hand, I don't feel that a date should discipline the single mother's child," asserts Art, the thirty-seven-year-old navy lieutenant. "In the first place, it is not his prerogative. The mother should take the responsibility. Further, since the man isn't around all of the time, such actions can be very confusing and upsetting to the child."

How Do They View the Children?

"Children should be an inseparable part of the single mother and, because of this, I always want to meet a woman's children early in the relationship," says Scott, forty-eight years old and a widower with grown children. "I know that children who are well behaved are also usually well loved and carefully guided by their mothers. When I meet children who look slovenly, who talk with food spewing out of their mouths, who drape themselves over chairs while a guest is present, and who talk back to their mother, I know that the mother cannot have been too involved in their lives.

"Does that sound unfair? Yes, it may be, and it is also selfish. I am a fairly well-off man, and I can afford many luxuries. When I am romantically involved with a woman, I want her to enjoy these luxuries with me, and the way I see it, where she goes her children should also go. If I see sloppy upbringing in her children, not only do I fear having them in public with me, but I also fear that I will soon learn that their mother is equally slovenly in her intellectual and emotional habits."

The speaker is a cultured and reserved man, as you can perceive from the above account. In spite of this facade, Scott has been found on numerous occasions racing a three-year-old in the pool—and letting her win. He has been seen playing catch with a six-year-old boy in a muddy field. And he has also been found curled up on the sofa, a child on each side of him, reading aloud with great delight.

There are other men like Scott who really like children, but they want them to be civilized rather than wild brutes. Most single mothers would also prefer to have their children act in a civilized manner. For some, however, the time and the effort that must be expended in providing children with the proper guidance cuts too deeply into more preferred activities. So they neglect to properly train their children.

"Children are little animals, and my experience in dating single mothers hasn't changed that opinion," observes Jon, thirty-eight years old and never-married. "I really don't want any children of my own, and that's one reason that I will probably wait until I am in my forties to marry. If I would marry now, even if I don't want my own children, the chances are good that the woman I'd marry will have children already. By the time the women are in their forties, their children will be grown, and I can then look toward marriage."

Not every man who dates the single mother concentrates on discipline, but many do mention it as the most glaring area of neglect regarding children. The failure to instill proper respect, control, and behavior in your children may be a major factor in the failure of a romantic relationship.

Children who run roughshod over their mothers receive a resounding "thumbs down" from men, as do children who act as if they have the final say in the activities of adults. Not surprisingly, these two dislikes are tied to proper discipline.

The news is not all negative. You will find that men often seek out single mothers as romantic partners because they are comforted by the possibility of a "ready-made" family. You may remember that the diaper stage of your child was all cuteness and cuddles, but men often see that stage as akin to house-breaking a dog, with all of the attendant problems.

"I think that children can make great companions, and there is something exciting about teaching them about the world surrounding them," says James, forty-two years old and divorced with no children. "I know that babies are cute and cuddly sometimes, but that's the stuff that mothers enjoy.

"I think that most men would agree that a child really becomes a companion to a man when he reaches the age of nine or ten and he really becomes curious about the whys of the world. I have also found that children of that age more readily become an active part of the relationship because baby-sitters and such aren't needed except when the mother and I are out in the evening."

With children, as with everything else, there are differences in the way that different men view the children of the single mothers that they date.

"Children about four or five years old are the oldest ones that I could really start with," says Ted, thirty-eight years old and never-married. "I'd be afraid that older children might be too difficult to control and to get to know. They already have their habits and ways of relating to people, and I'd be competition for their mother. How would they react to me?"

Perhaps that last question is behind a lot of the hesitancy that men feel about getting to know the children of the single mother. Men may have a natural aversion to children, or they may make a big case for discipline. Under it all, however, there may be the lingering concern, the lingering fear, that they may not measure up to the expectations of the children.

The Difficulties of Dating Single Mothers

"Single mothers are like any other woman," says Ari, forty-seven years old and divorced three times with four children. "There are no difficulties with dating single mothers. You meet them, you are attracted, and you start to date. All a woman has to have is good child care, and then the relationship can proceed like any other."

All the woman has to have is good child care, you say? All she has to have is a house staff of ten. All she has to do is win $10 million in the lottery. Ari's suggestion is highly unrealistic in light of the many child-care problems that the average single mother must confront. More realistic is the man who will admit difficulties.

"It would be great if we could stay out all night or jet to Paris, or even to Omaha on the new low plane fares," jokes Ben, fifty-seven years old and a widower with grown children. "But we can't, and that's fine because a woman's children should have her home at night. I don't mind going home with her, either.

"But seriously now, you have to admit that there are only a certain number of hours allotted to you through the grace of grandmothers and baby-sitters, then a woman has to get home. Ice, snow, and a warm bed shouldn't prevent her from going home at the hour that she promised her baby-sitter that she would return. To make today's baby-sitters wait too late can spell the end of the sitter's availability. Finding good sitters isn't easy, or so I gather."

The Mistakes Single Mothers Make

1. *Discipline.* The major complaint of men who have dated single mothers is that single mothers do not discipline their children properly. Dinner at a restaurant turns into a horrifying experience as children talk with their mouths full, grab at food, talk back to the adults, and create havoc at the table. At home, badly behaved children refuse to help their mothers, they are slovenly, and they are rude and abusive to their mothers.

   When single mothers do exercise some authority, their children are likely to ignore them because there is little consistency in their discipline. In the attempt to make up for their earlier leniency, men note, mothers try to be overly restrictive when they do discipline. This lack of consistency not only confuses the child, but it also renders ineffective any attempts at discipline.

2. *Moving too fast.* Men who enter a relationship with a single mother may very well have the intention of a lifelong commitment, but they may also just want to enjoy a short-term relationship with no intentions for a future. Still, say many men, the single mothers that they've dated frequently begin planning on the first date.

   Before they are even sure of a second date, many women will begin to suggest places and activities that they can all share together. Further, note these men, they often feel trapped when a woman introduces them too early in the relationship to their children. An uncomfortable side effect of these introductions is the tendency of single mothers to tell their dates afterward that their young children have asked if they will be their "new daddies."

3. *Expecting men to play the role of surrogate father.* Men don't dislike the role of big brother, confidant, or adviser, but taking on the role of surrogate father is too emotionally laden for some men. The divorced man who does not have custody of his children will avoid too close a relationship with the single mother's children, if he can, because he feels guilt over his own children. The never-married man may feel uncomfortable with children who are forced upon him. The widower may have his hands full with his own children.

   Rather than expecting a man to play a role with your children, suggest men, you should allow such relationships to develop gradually. Introduce your children when it feels comfortable, then let the man make the next move.

4. *Keeping the man an outsider in the relationship between the single mother and her children.* In contrast to the men who feel that single mothers too frequently rush the relationship between their children and a man, there are many men who feel left out. They complain that some single mothers are too wrapped up in their children and that the closed nature of the mother-child relationship keeps them an outsider looking in.

   The way to meet this criticism, and that voiced above, is to remain sensitive to the signals sent out by the man you date. If a man seems to honestly want to get to know your children, and if the suggestions to spend time with your children come from him, you should bring your child into the relationship and bring your man into the mother-child relationship to the extent it is comfortable all around.

5. *Expecting the man to pay for everything.* Divorced men who are paying child support often find that they can live fairly well, but too many expensive dates will drain them financially. Widowers who are solely responsible for the mental and physical well-being of their children may also be financially strapped. When the single mother and her children join the divorced man or widower on an outing, the result can be costly.

   Although they will occasionally pay for activities and meals, many divorced men and widowers with children feel that the mother should be responsible for paying the way for her children. Burgers are expensive, and admission to amusement parks and movies can be exorbitant. Even when they fully welcome the presence of the single mother's children, many men find that they will pull back if the cost in dollars may be too high.

These five are the major complaints that men voice about their relationships with single mothers and their children. Several other "mistakes" have also been mentioned, with varying degrees of frequency. Although they may plague individual men, these "mistakes" are not among the issues that make men avoid dating single mothers.

1. Asking a man to play the role of handyman in your home after only a date or two.
2. Suggesting that your children and her children get together for a "sleepover" or other activity, a tactic seen as trying to entrap the man.
3. Using sex to barter.
4. Expressing little interest in sex.
5. Complaining about your money problems and trying to borrow money from a man.
6. Asking a man to pay your bills, "just this once."
7. Having your children send a man cute, father-type cards on his birthday, for Father's Day, and on other holidays.
8. Insisting that a man and his children come to family functions with the extended family.
9. Talking with his children in the effort to find out about his love life and his financial situation.
10. Moaning about the sad lot of the single mother.

Are you guilty of any of these mistakes? That may not matter one way or another with some men, because these actions of the single mother do not bother all men. Still, you can never be sure how the man that you're dating feels about what you may see as a perfectly normal way to run your life as a single mother. Before you begin to analyze your life and feel guilty for your "mistakes," remember that you must live your life in a way that pleases you. If you want to change something because you find that it is no longer tolerable in your life, fine. If, however, you change simply to please someone else, then consider what you will do when that "someone else" is no longer a part of your life.

18

Some Warning Signs for Single Mothers About Lovers Who May Be Dangerous to Their Children

"You have one chance with your children, and you can never get a second chance," says Stacy, the forty-five-year-old divorced mother of a teenage daughter. "I almost lost my chance with Sandra because of Milt. I never thought that he would try to hurt my daughter in that way. He's a grown man, and a good partner in bed. Why would he try to force himself on a thirteen-year-old girl who has never done anything to give him any indication that she was inviting such behavior? I don't understand."

Stacy's disbelief stems from a recent incident in which her lover of over a year forced her young daughter to let him fondle her while her mother wasn't home. Although Milt had been alone in the house with Sandra for brief periods of time in the past, he had never done anything like this before. His defense was that he was under great strain at work and "something just snapped." Stacy isn't going to press charges, but she has packed up all of Milt's belongings and told him to leave. She is now mourning for her daughter's frightening experience and for her own betrayed love.

Child molestation is a big fear among single mothers with young children, but it isn't the only problem that single mothers face when they begin to bring men home. Single mothers with young children, as well as those with grown children, must choose their partners carefully. Even if your children are no longer impressionable, they may still be emotionally hurt by contact with a man who resents their claim on your life.

Once you begin to date, your life and home are opened to new people and new experiences. These can be beneficial to your children or they may produce negative impressions that remain for life. The responsibility for making certain that these new experiences are positive for your children lies with you.

Sex Abuse and Your Child

You shouldn't take anything for granted regarding your child's safety. Although you may want to trust a man who treats you well as an adult woman, you cannot assume that he will not endanger your children when you are not around. As Dr. Victor Solomon warns, "You can't afford to be careless with your child. Even a relatively brief incident can enter and remain in the subconscious. A misplaced hand, a fondle, these actions enter the child's subconscious and turn up in later life as early episodes of sexual abuse that have had a negative effect on the child's life."

A single mother should be selective and observant about her partner. Your son or daughter should not have to be afraid to be alone in the same room with the man you are dating, nor should they have to constantly monitor their own behavior to make certain that nothing they say is provocative.

You have the responsibility of scrutinizing your dates carefully before placing your children unprotected in their company. Make certain that you know a man well before you trust him with the most valuable part of your life—your child.

It may come as a surprise to single mothers who pick their men with care, but not every woman is absolutely sure of the character of the man that she is dating. This is especially true of women who frequently date men that they've met casually and about whom they know next to nothing. If this is your dating pattern, then you are taking chances with your own safety by dating these men. When you bring them home, however, you begin to take chances with the safety of your child.

It is a sad fact that single mothers must face, nonetheless, that some men specifically choose to date single mothers with the intention of getting at their young children.

A pedophile has patience. Pedophiles have been known to spend years building up the confidence of an organization in order to be placed in a position that will allow them direct and easy access to young children. Gaining access through a single mother is a much easier task.

"The ad should have raised my suspicions," says Carla tearfully, recalling the personal ad that first brought her into contact with the man who molested her eight-year-old daughter. "He wrote that he was 'a never-married bachelor in his forties, looking for the right woman and an already-begun family.' I was just divorced and feeling very low. That ad really came when I was very vulnerable. It promised love and acceptance, and it gave me hope that someone would want me and my child after all.

"I answered the ad and included my telephone number. When he called, I was impressed by Fred's mannerly tone and the pleasant sound of his voice. I agreed to meet him for coffee and to bring Missy with me.

"He seemed so nice. He spoke about having nursed his ill mother until she died recently. That seemed to account for his having never married. He complimented me on my daughter and told me that she was very pretty. During our talk, he frequently directed his conversation to Missy, making her feel very grown up, and he looked at her warmly throughout the conversation.

"The crazy thing is that his behavior actually made me feel secure inside! I thought to myself, now here is a man who will love both me and my little girl. It wouldn't be like the horror stories that I had heard from other single mothers who had found that men often blocked their children out entirely or treated their children coldly. Oh, God, was I wrong.

"We began to date, and we went out every Friday evening, then spent Saturday evenings at my home playing board games with Missy or watching TV. Fred would carry her up to her room at bedtime, then linger to tell her a story. I stayed out of this quiet time because I wanted so much for them to get along. I wanted to be married again, and Fred seemed like a good choice.

"Those bedtimes haunt me now. In therapy, Missy has revealed that Fred would fondle her and have her touch him in the genital area. She knew that something was wrong, but she, too, was afraid of saying anything that might drive Fred away. She was so hungry for a full-time father.

"I should have seen what was happening. How could I miss the signs? And to think that I was so happy that he was so interested in her, that he seemed to like her even more than me.

"That Saturday night would never have happened if I had focused more on building an adult relationship with a man and less on just finding a spouse at all cost. What a price Missy paid.

"I ran out to a 'five-hour sale' at the mall and left Missy and Fred alone to play their usual board games. Missy was a little clingy, but I thought that she was just tired from the day, so I told Fred to put her to bed early.

"When I returned three hours later, Missy was cowering in her bedroom, blood on her nightgown. Fred was gone. The police picked him up a few hours later and charged him. He had been picked up for similar violations in the past, but had managed to escape imprisonment through one means or another. I vowed that he would be punished this time, and I pressed charges.

"Missy is now ten, and her therapy appears to be working, but she still shivers when a grown man comes too near to her. I haven't dated since that happened. Why did I let it happen?"

Carla's grief is still fresh, even two years after the unfortunate incident. Her decision to refrain from dating, however, is doing more to hurt Missy than she may realize because she is reinforcing Missy's fear of men through her own avoidance of them. She is punishing herself for the pain that Missy suffered by cutting herself off from men. In the process, she is keeping Missy from knowing that all men are not like Fred. Missy must be given the opportunity to know men who are gentle, loving, kind, and psychologically normal. By dating such men, Carla can help her daughter to heal more fully and to accept men once again.

Are there any signs that will give you some warning that your lover may be dangerous to your children? Yes, say the experts, and these are signs that you should not ignore.

1. You should be suspicious if your lover focuses his main attention on your children and not on you. Although he may be trying to please you by becoming friendly with your child, too much of this should make you suspicious. Watch carefully how he acts with you when the two of you are alone. Does his conversation focus mainly on your child? Does he avoid physical intimacy with you? Is he often impatient to leave you once your child is out of your company?

2. Don't allow a new date or even a long-time lover to fondle your children, even nonsexually, or kiss your children on the lips.

3. Be suspicious if a new date suggests quite soon after meeting you that he take your child off alone on outings or that he take the child to his place for a while to allow you some rest.

4. Watch for sexually charged remarks that are directed at your children, both preadolescent and adolescent. It is one thing to remark that a young girl is going to be a "real doll" when she grows up, and quite another to remark that a young girl is "going to have some body" when she grows up.

5. Avoid men who abuse alcohol or drugs, both of which are often used as excuses for a range of antisocial behaviors, including child molesting.

6. Be alert if your date or lover asks your child to model a skimpy piece of clothing or undergarment.

7. Stop all contact with a man who implies a fascination with the bodies of young children or who possesses any form of child pornography.

You are the protector of your children. To keep them safe, you should screen carefully the men that you bring home. Take a careful look at the men who will enter your children's lives. Pay close attention to their drinking habits, their ability to control anger, the way in which they interact with you as an adult female. Unless your children will be safely out of the house,

don't bring home a man whose personal characteristics or behavior make you feel even slightly uncomfortable. For that
matter, why take such risks yourself?

Listen to Your Children

In spite of all of your precautions, an incident might still occur
that will make your child frightened and fearful of telling you.
If your child does brave telling you that your lover has been
making indecent suggestions or advances, reassure him or her
that telling you was the right way to handle it.

Then get to the bottom of the situation immediately. Confront your lover with the charge, and watch carefully for his
reaction.

Your child is very precious, and even one act of sexual
abuse can leave its mark forever. Your child does not deserve
that punishment.

The chances are great that your son or daughter will be
afraid to tell you about a sexual advance or a fondling incident
because they may feel that you will not believe them. It will be
their word against your lover's.

You can offset the possibility of this happening by speaking
with all of your children about sexual abuse. Warn them that
even people close to them may do something that makes them
feel uncomfortable. Just because a person is close to them doesn't
make the act right.

What kinds of gestures and touching should a child report
to you? The answer is anything that makes your child feel
uncomfortable. A child should be taught that some touches by
others are appropriate and that other touches are not. Some
touches make us feel warm and loved, but other touches make
us feel uncomfortable and frightened. Hugs are not good if they
invade the child's personal comfort level and if they demand
lengthy and inappropriate body contact.

This is a point at which the nature of your relationship
with your children becomes very important. You have to speak
openly with your children about their bodies, about their rights
to their own bodies, and about the ways in which others may
make inappropriate claims on their bodies.

This is best done when you have the time to answer the
many questions that your child will probably raise. It is also a

very good idea to tell your child, and casually to reinforce this frequently, that you are always willing to answer his questions and to listen when he has something, even something "embarrassing," to tell you.

You should reassure your children that no matter who has sexually harassed them, they can always come to you for comfort and protection. This is very important because most children do not report the first attempts, and this simply makes the molester more brazen and more dangerous to your child.

Men to Avoid

Men who have a history of abusing children, sexually or otherwise, should be at the top of your list of men to avoid. These should be closely followed by men whose behavior with your children gives you a feeling or evidence that they have an inappropriate interest in your child.

In addition to potential molesters, there are other men who can do your child harm. Men with volatile tempers who destroy objects when angry or who rant and rave over the slightest perceived injustice are better left alone. Your child doesn't need to experience such potentially damaging behavior in someone who may become close to you if the relationship should continue.

These men are the more obvious types to avoid because their overt behavior gives them away. There are others whose negative traits are less obvious but who will do substantial damage to your child's development if they are in frequent contact.

Psychotherapist Dr. Marge Steinfeld warns single mothers against dating the following types of men who can interfere with your child's normal emotional growth and development:

1. Any man who has a great need for all of Mom's attention is a bad choice. If he seems jealous and unable to share either people or material items with others, watch out. A man of this sort is looking for a mother. He is a dependent person who will be nothing more than another sibling to your children, and a jealous one at that.

2. Any man who shows any unfavorable personality traits such as being physically or verbally abusive, poking fun at a child, harshness, or erratic behavior. A person who shows no interest in connecting and a man who is too rigid are also poor choices as a date for the single mother.

The responsibility for keeping your children safe and for assuring that they are given the appropriate opportunity for mental and physical growth lies with you. It may seem to be a heavy burden to manage, but it is one that you should assume willingly. You can't afford to bring men into your life who will endanger your children physically, emotionally, or mentally. Your children are too important, and they have the right to be protected.

These precautions should not be viewed as placing restraints on your choice of men, rather they are guidelines in selecting men who will be good for both you and your children. Childhood is brief, but the damage to a child who has experienced child abuse of one kind or another can last a lifetime. The regrets of being careless with the well-being of a child will surely last forever.

19

What Is Ahead in the Next Decade for the Single Mother?

The next decade promises to be exciting for single mothers and their children. The divorce rate, coupled with a greater number of women who are choosing to have their children without being married, will result in greater numbers of single mothers than ever before. These increased numbers are certain to create changes that will profoundly increase the quality of life for the single mother in the United States.

Certainly, single mothers of the near future are likely to be better educated and more secure in their careers than today's single mothers. Whether they have learned from the experiences of this generation of women or if their drive to succeed first and parent later is just stronger is not certain. Nonetheless, many young women today are establishing themselves in careers and completing their education before marrying and having children. As a result, they can look to the future with greater self-confidence and earning power and a resilience that will be passed on to their children.

The increased visibility of single mothers will have another, more significant, result. As most special-interest groups have found, and as single mothers are discovering, strength is to be found in the ballot box and through lobbying. Single mothers have primarily been a fragmented group, divided in their concerns along economic, regional, and cultural lines. Urbanites had different concerns than suburbanites, and they each tended their concerns in an isolated manner. Today, however, there is a growing awareness that we share many of the same concerns as all other single mothers, whether we live in Los Angeles, New York City, or Angola, Indiana. This awareness is being translated into organized efforts that will benefit all single mothers.

Changing Trends in Society

The single mother will enjoy a greater acceptance in the future as the number of women raising children alone due to divorce and single motherhood by choice increases. The tendency of some women professionals to feel their "biological time clock" ticking away has resulted in their choosing to have children without having a husband to complicate their lives. Making such a choice a decade ago would have spelled certain disaster for a woman's career in most instances, and it is still a risky, even dangerous decision for today's career woman who wants to be taken seriously for a top job with a company.

Still, as women continue to show greater dedication to careers, postponing marriage until their mid- or late thirties, those who want to have children will have to make choices. Because the majority of men in the late twenties to mid-forties age group are usually married, the choices for professional women who marry late are greatly narrowed. Unless women who aim for motherhood are willing to enter into marriages with men significantly older or younger, many will most likely choose to go it alone.

These professionals who become single mothers will be a viable force in changing the way that our nation views day care. They will be joined by other single mothers who are of an increasingly higher education level, to make demands of business and the government that will make quality day care the right of every single mother.

At present, day care and the problems of the working single mother are low-priority items for government spending. Companies throughout our nation have begun to test the value of on-site day-care centers for single parents, and although the results are not completely in, there are reports of greater productivity and greater worker satisfaction after the installation of these centers.

Such embryonic efforts will be greatly expanded in the future as a result of lobbying by single mothers for better facilities for their children and more extensive benefits for themselves. To date, media exposure of the difficulties that single mothers face in obtaining quality day care for their children has focused attention on the issue.

Future single mothers and their children will become the prime movers in efforts to reform the way in which both business and government view the needs of working single mothers. In the past, when women employees were viewed as working to provide only supplemental income, when women were seen as less than serious about careers, employers could more easily dismiss the concerns and needs of female employees. Absenteeism by mothers, single or otherwise, was seen as being part of some vaguely defined female problem that included pregnancy and monthly cramps. It was also viewed as providing evidence that women weren't as serious about work as men.

Growing numbers of women in the workplace, growing numbers of female decision makers, and growing numbers of women in the political arena are beginning to refute and to dispute these assumptions. As women begin to play ever-greater roles in running the machinery of both business and government, they are making their needs known with ever-louder voices. A significant number of these women are single mothers who have found that there is strength in numbers.

Legislators and lawmakers will pay greater attention to the concerns of single mothers as they begin to recognize their voting power. Today's figure of five million single mothers surely will grow, and many children of single mothers will be reaching voting age in the next decade. The combined voting power of single mothers and their children could comprise a formidable political force.

We will see change in other social institutions as a result of the greater numbers of single mothers and adults who were raised in single-mother families. Schools have already begun considering a lengthened school day in order to correspond more closely with the work day. The effort may not be pleasing to all children, but it has been suggested in the effort to eliminate the large number of "latchkey" children who often go home to empty homes and who must remain alone for hours.

Several other options are currently being explored by school systems around the country. Motivated by the growing number of mothers who work, and the large percentage of single-mother-headed families, educators have suggested that mandatory schooling begin at the age of four rather than the present five years of age. In addition, studies are being conducted into the feasibility of year-round schooling that would permit more detailed learning by children which would eliminate the difficulty of finding appropriate care for children during the summer months. Both proposals are still in the exploratory stage, but working mothers, both married and single, have endorsed these options. In the next decade, we may find that one or both options have become well-accepted procedures of our nation's system of public education.

Although such extensive changes will take years to implement, changes are already being seen in individual schools because of the larger percentage of single mothers who are administrators and educators, as well as those who have children in the schools. A new sensitivity to the children has emerged.

Instead of parent activities that emphasize both parents, or that emphasize one (such as "Father's Night" or "Mother's Night"), the schools are slowly shifting to the recognition that many children can't supply both parents. They are often lucky that one exists to attend functions.

Changing Trends in Relationships

Relationships in the United States have changed considerably in the last few years, and the single mother has found herself in the mainstream of society. Formerly unwilling to talk about being divorced or never-married, and shy of reentering a social life if widowed, she is now a major topic of conversation and speculation and an increasingly important and influential voice in our culture and our state and national politics.

A revolution has occurred among single mothers that promises to change the image of the single mother and the self-perceptions of her children forever. These changes, which began in the last decade, should exert an important influence as we move rapidly toward the twenty-first century.

The trend in recent years has been for women to achieve higher levels of education, either before marrying or after becoming single mothers. Media coverage of one or another mother who has gone back to school to either complete a degree or to initiate an education that she could never before obtain is now commonplace. This means that the single mother of today is generally better educated than her predecessors, and her children are being raised by women who are developing a better understanding of the workings of the world around them.

The trend toward higher levels of education will continue, and as a result, women who may become single mothers in the future will be more articulate spokeswomen for their group. They are also more likely to be deeply involved in professions that not only will provide them with great personal satisfaction but also with substantial financial compensation. Contrary to the low wages paid in general to women, those women who have professional degrees and whose expertise is in areas of greatest need are making salaries that are competitive with men's.

The importance of the increased education and better financial stability of single mothers is that fewer will be eager or forced to remarry strictly for economic reasons, still a major reason that single mothers remarry. Unlike the past, when a single mother considered herself lucky to have a man marry her and raise her children, the single mother of the future is preparing now to raise her own children and under the best circumstances possible.

This expectation will change the character of male-female relationships because more than simple economic necessity will be the criteria that the single mother will use in determining whether or not she will remarry.

Such changes are already influencing the values of today's young men; older men are learning to cope with the new confidence and assertiveness of the single mother. In the past, the man who married a single mother became her protector, her provider, and a father to her child. She was grateful for having been rescued, and he became a hero. Many such marriages were happy, and children thrived under the tutelage of their stepfathers.

There were also many such marriages in which the rescuer soon became the tyrant, never letting his wife forget that she should be grateful that he was paying her way and that of her child. The balance of power, already determined by a woman's lack of earning power, was tipped further in the man's favor by his having assumed the "burden" of her child.

This inequity still exists, and many single mothers continue to find that economic (rather than emotional) considerations motivate them to marry. The good news is that the greater self-confidence and the greater ability to survive on their own has decreased the number of single mothers who marry out of economic necessity. A woman who is able to earn a living and who has a healthy sense of her own worth is likely to demand more than a paycheck from a man. She is also likely to demand more in a potential surrogate father for her child.

This new and strengthened position of single mothers means that the men who date them must be able to offer more than just a financially secure future. Because single mothers who are doing well with their children do not have to "settle" for just anyone, men who may marry them will have to be more than just adequate—as both potential husbands and fathers. This requirement places pressure on younger men, who may not have had experience in raising a child. It can also be frightening to the older man who has grown up with an outdated view of single mothers and who may now wonder if he is capable of meeting the standards of today's assertive and self-confident single mother and her ready-made family.

Men will be strongly influenced by the growing number of single mothers. Not only will contact with single mothers and their families sensitize them in many ways, but many more men in the next decades will have lived at least a part of their lives as children of single mothers. Sociologists observe that over half of the children today will live alone with their mothers for at least some period in their lives. This experience will have far-reaching effects on the way in which men will view the family unit, and it will also influence the manner in which women, even those who spend all of their youth in intact families, view marriage and the family unit.

For some children, having shared in the experience of the single mother will affect their view of marriage and fatherhood. As one nine-year-old boy, the son of a single mother, has said after considering his own future, "I'm going to be real careful before I get married, and I'm going to try very hard to be with my children when they're very little."

The coming decade will be a time of change for the better, as single mothers become stronger, more self-reliant individuals who will lead their children bravely into the twenty-first century. Should they choose a relationship, it will be on theirs and their children's terms, and not because there is nowhere else to turn.

Recommended Reading

Atlas, Stephen L. *Parents Without Partners Sourcebook.* Philadelphia: Running Press, 1984.

Atlas, Stephen L. *Single Parenting: A Practical Resource Guide.* Englewood Cliffs, NJ: Prentice-Hall, 1981.

Barnes, Beverly C., and Coplon, Jennifer. *The Single Parent Experience: A Time for Growth.* New York: Family Service America, 1980.

Barnes, Robert G. *Single Parenting: A Wilderness Journey.* Wheaton, IL: Tyndale Press, 1984.

Caine, Lynn. *Widow.* New York: Bantam Books, 1975.

Carter, Velma T., and Leavenworth, J. Lynn. *Putting the Pieces Together.* Valley Forge, PA: Judson Press, 1977.

Cashmore, Ernest. *Having To: The World of One Parent Families.* Winchester, MA: Allen Unwin, Inc., 1985.

Clarke, Clara, and Mahone, Stella. *Coping Alone: How to Be a Successful Single Parent.* Riverside, NJ: M. Boyars, 1986.

Curto, Josephine. *How to Become a Single Parent; A Guide for Single People Considering Adoption or Natural Parenthood Alone.* Englewood Cliffs, NJ: Prentice-Hall, 1983.

Dolmetssch, Paul, and Shih, Alexa. *Kid's Book about Single Parent Families.* New York: Doubleday & Co., 1985.

Durland, Frances C. *Coping with Widowhood.* Liguori, MO: Liguori Publications, 1979.

Fabisch, Judith. *A Widow's Guide to Living Alone.* Grand Rapids, MI: Zondervan Publishers, 1983.

Fisher, Ida, and Lane, Byron. *The Widow's Guide to Life: How to Adjust— How to Grow.* Englewood Cliffs, NJ: Prentice-Hall, 1983.

Glick, Ira O., et al. *The First Year of Bereavement.* New York: John Wiley and Sons, 1974.

Horner, Catherine T. *The Single Parent Family in Children's Books: An Analysis and Annotated Bibliography.* Metuchen, NJ: Scarecrow Press, 1978.

Jensen, Marilyn. *Formerly Married: Learning to Live with Yourself.* Philadelphia: Westminster Publishing, 1983.

Klein, Carole. *The Single Parent Experience.* New York: Avon Books, 1973.

Kurtz, Eleanor. *What a Widow Needs to Know: A Guide for Widows and Helpers.* Saratoga, CA: R & E Publications, 1982.

LeShan, Eda. *What's Going to Happen to Me? When Parents Separate or Divorce.* New York: Scholastic, 1978.

Lindsay, Jeanne W. *Do I Have a Daddy? A Story About a Single-Parent Child with a Special Section for Single Mothers and Fathers.* Buena Park, CA: Morning Glory Press, 1982.

Lopata, H.Z. *Women as Widows: Support Systems.* Westport, CT: Greenwood Publishing, 1979.

McNamara, Lynne, and Morrison, Jennifer. *Separation, Divorce and After.* New York: University of Queensland Press, 1983.

Makris, Barbara, and Devis-Debeuneure, Linda. *Parenting: A Curriculum for the Single Working Mother.* Washington, DC: WOW, Inc., 1983.

Marindin, Hope, ed. *The Handbook for Single Adoptive Parents.* Chevy Chase, MD: The Committee for Single Adoptive Parents, 1985.

Mattis, Mary. *Sex and the Single Parent.* New York: Henry Holt, 1986.

Nudel, Adele Rice. *Starting Over: Help for Young Widows & Widowers.* New York: Dodd, Mead & Company, 1986.

Nye, Miriam B. *But I Never Thought He'd Die: Practical Help for Widows.* Philadelphia: Westminster Publishing, 1978.

Peppler, Alice S. *Single Again—This Time with Children: A Christian Guide for the Single Parent.* Augsburg, MN: Augsburg Publishing House, 1982.

Renvoize, Jean. *Going Solo: Single Mothers by Choice.* Boston: Routledge and Kegan Paul, Inc., 1985.

Rodgers, Joan, and Catalado, Michael F. *Raising Sons: Practical Strategies for Single Mothers.* New York: New American Library, 1984.

Silverman, Phyllis. *Widow-to-Widow.* New York: Springer Publishing, 1985.

Stewart, Suzanne. *Parent Alone.* Waco, TX: Word Books, 1978.

Taves, Isabella. *The Widow's Guide: Practical Advice on How to Deal with Grief, Stress, Health, Children and Family, Money, Work and Finally, Getting Back into the World.* New York: Schocken Books, 1981.

Weiss, Robert S. *Going It Alone: The Family Life and Social Situation of the Single Parent.* New York: Basic Books, 1981.

Index

A

Advice, from friends, 9
Affection, displays of, in front of
children, 134–35, 183
Age
    availability of men and, 59–62
    influence of children and, 64–65
    living arrangements and, 64
    sources of romantic involvement
        and, 62–64
Age-appropriate dressing, 124
AIDS (Acquired Immune Deficiency
    Syndrome)
    one-night stands and, 23, 26, 36
    short affairs and, 27
Appointment book, need for, 125
Availability of men, and age, 59–62

B

Babysitters, 125–26
Battle of the sexes, 120
Binge, sexual, 35–36

C

Celibacy
    benefits of, 155
    as a choice, 153–54
    definition of, 152–53
    explaining reasons for, 154–55
    length of, 159–61
    and masturbation, 155–56
    men's reaction to, 157–59
    reaction of other women to, 155
Child-care arrangements, 125–26
Children
    age of, effect of dating on,
        132–34
    awareness of mother's sexual
        activity, 139
    babysitters, 125–26
    blaming children for lack of
        meeting men, 8
    child-care arrangements, 125–26
    closeness to lover, 149
    competition between mother and
        daughter, 128–29
    displays of affection and, 134–35,
        183
    divorced man and, 104–106
    effect of dating married man on,
        117
    effect of dating never-married
        man on, 110–11
    effect of dating on, 117,127–35
    flaunting sexual activity and, 137
    grown children, 139–43, 183–85
    grown daughters, 141–43
    grown sons, 140
    and guilt of new relationships, 51
    influence of, and age, 64–65
    introducing into relationship, 127,
        167–68
    latchkey, 203–204
    live-at-home children and sex,
        137–39
    living arrangements, repercussions
        of, 64
    making child feel secure, 182–83
    meeting too many men, 134
    men's meeting of, 127
    men's view of, 189–91
    older, 133–34
    and questions about fathers, 55
    reaction to younger man, 114
    role in romance, 7–9
    and sexual abuse, 196–202
    sexual activity as disturbance to,
        138–39
    unmarried grown daughters,
        142–43
    view of mother's dating, 175–85
    widowed men and, 106–108
    widowed mother, reaction to
        dating, 46, 47
    younger men and, 114
Child support, 172, 193
Closeness
    of children to lover, 149
    emotional desire for, 151
Commitment, 29–31
    meaning of, 163
    possibilities of, 163–66
    proper time for, 162–63
    questions about, 171

Ex-husband
  effect on freedom to date, 37–38
  as peeping-Tom, 39–41
  reaction to former wife's dating,
    39–40
  remarriage of, 40–41
Expectations
  meeting others, 12
  of sexual favors, 154

F

Family, introductions through, 96
Fears
  of admitting readiness for
    romantic involvement, 16
  of the future, 151
  of trying, 32–33
Financial obligations, in new
  household, 172–73
Formal matchmaking, 96
Free time, 151
Friends
  feelings toward single life style,
    14
  gay male, 83–85
  introductions through, 96
  and resumption of social life, 7,
    10
  straight male, 85–87

G

Gay men
  falling in love with, 84–85
  as friends, 83–85
Going It Alone (Weiss), 8
Grieving process, following death or
  divorce, 160–61
Grown daughters
  effect of mother's dating on,
    183–85
  resistance to mother's sex life,
    139–43
Grown sons
  effect of mother's dating on,
    183–85
  lover as threat to, 141
  and mother's sex life, 139–43

as protectors, 140
Guilt
  of dating as a widow, 46
  induced by others, 41
  of new relationships, 51

H

Happiness, of single motherhood,
  10–11, 14–15
Herpes
  and one-night stands, 23, 26, 36
  and short affairs, 27
Holidays, and the single mother, 13

I

Intimacy, 12
  privacy and, 143–47

J

Jealousy
  child's, 179
  of unmarried grown daughters,
    142–43

L

Latchkey children, 203–204
Liberated men, 78–80
  "truly liberated" men, 87–88
Living arrangements, 164–65
  and age, 64
  changing, 148
  invasion of living space, 165
  live-ins, 147–49
  and repercussions for children, 64
Loneliness, 12–13, 151
Long-term relationships
  living arrangements, 148
  and sexual activity, 139
  versus short affairs, 29

M

Macho men, 76–77
Marriage
  effect on family unit, 166
  reservations about, 31